HOW TO MAKE SLIPCOVERS

Designing, Measuring, and Sewing Perfect-Fit
Slipcovers for Chairs, Sofas, and Ottomans

Patricia Hoskins

Storey Publishing

NS

3064514619554

*The mission of Storey Publishing is to serve our customers by
publishing practical information that encourages
personal independence in harmony with the environment.*

Edited by Nancy D. Wood and Melinda A. Slaving
Series design by Alethea Morrison
Art direction by Jeff Stiefel and Michaela Jebb
Text production by Theresa Wiscovitch
Indexed by Christine R. Lindemer, Boston Road Communications

Cover illustration by © Ashley Le Quere
Interior illustrations by Allegra Lockstadt

Storey Publishing
210 MASS MoCA Way
North Adams, MA 01247
www.storey.com

Printed in the United States by McNaughton & Gunn, Inc.
10 9 8 7 6 5 4 3 2 1

LIBRARY OF CONGRESS CATALOGING-IN-PUBLICATION DATA

Hoskins, Patricia.
   How to make slipcovers : designing, measuring, and sewing perfect-fit slipcovers for
   chairs, sofas, and ottomans / Patricia Hoskins.
      pages cm
   ISBN 978-1-61212-525-1 (pbk. : alk. paper)
   ISBN 978-1-61212-526-8 (ebook) 1. Slip covers. I. Title.
TT395.H67 2015
646.2'1—dc23
                              2015009441

CONTENTS

CHAPTER ONE

SLIPCOVER DESIGN AND ASSEMBLY

Before embarking on any new adventure, I like to have at least a rough plan in place — whether I stick to it or not! This chapter contains a step-by-step guide to the slipcovering process, from obtaining materials and equipment to the finished product. I've organized this book to follow the Step-by-Step Overview, on the next page, as closely as possible, though there are a few exceptions here and there. I also review what types of equipment and supplies you'll want to have on hand to create a successful and sturdy slipcover.

STEP-BY-STEP OVERVIEW

WHETHER YOU OWN dated furniture that needs a bit of a make-over or prized newer pieces that need some protection from the "elements" in your house (particularly those pesky pets and kids!), a slipcover is one of the simplest and most effective ways to protect your furnishings while refreshing the look of your home at the same time.

Slipcovers can range from the simplest option — a length of fabric draped over a chair or sofa, tied in place at strategic points (or not!) — to the most complex fitted and tailored cover, almost indistinguishable from a completely reupholstered piece. In any case, the key feature of a slipcover is that it can be easily removed for laundering or replaced with another slipcover for a completely different look.

One caveat: Do be aware that slipcovers can't fix or hide all sins that might be found in your furniture. If your piece has a bad odor or if the stuffing is worn or lumpy, you will probably want to consider a complete overhaul and reupholstery.

Let's take a look at the steps covered in this book, with page references that tell you where to look for each bit of information.

1. Stock your supplies (pages 2–7).

2. Make an initial shopping trip to evaluate fibers and fabrics available (pages 11–15). Purchase swatches and test them by stitching through four layers. Verify the width, pattern repeat size (pages 9–11), and yardage availability of favorite(s).

3. Measure the furniture and determine pattern pieces (chapter 5, page 36). Record the dimensions in the measuring charts provided in chapter 5 and add any seam allowances needed.

4. Select styling details to determine additional allowances required: skirt style and allowances (pages 64–74), hem style (pages 74–77), and trim placement and type (pages 29–32).

5. Estimate base yardage requirements (chapter 7, page 82).

6. Draft cutting layout. Include cushion covers, welting, skirt, and piecing allowances in the cutting layout as needed. Calculate total yardage requirements based on fabric width (page 84) and pattern repeat allowances (page 87).

7. Purchase muslin, fabric, and trims. Prewash/pretreat fabrics and trims as needed.

8. Make any and all welting as desired (pages 18–24).

9. Cut body panels out of muslin.

10. Fit, pin, mark, and baste muslin patterns (pages 94–96). Make any final adjustments to the pattern pieces and seams as needed, and mark all changes clearly.

11. Disassemble muslin. Cut pieces from final fabric, matching repeats if necessary (page 88).

12. Baste welting to fabric seam allowances (pages 29–30).

13. Fit and assemble final slipcover (page 94–97).

14. Make and attach the skirt (chapter 6, page 64).

15. Install zipper closure as desired (pages 113–117).

MATERIALS AND TOOLS

WHEN CREATING YOUR CUSTOM SLIPCOVERS, you will need a large table and workspace. Nothing can beat having enough room to work! Remember that slipcovers can be very large, both the individual pattern pieces and the finished cover!

Materials

In addition to selecting fabric for your slipcovers (see chapter 2, page 8), you want to equip yourself with the proper supplies.

Muslin. Use this inexpensive fabric to create sample pattern pieces for testing and fitting your slipcover.

Upholstery thread. While this type of thread is the best for stitching slipcovers, some sewing machines can protest, even after adjusting tension, bobbin, and needle size. For an alternative, try *corespun* (also known as *polycore, cottoncore,* or *core thread*) or topstitch thread, both of which are stronger than all-purpose thread.

Trim. If making your own welting, you'll need cable cording or filler cord in the determined width and yardage (see page 18). If you prefer to buy ready-made trim, look for commercial welting, fringe, or other trim. These come with a built-in *flange,* or tape, ready to be sewn into the seams of your slipcovers. If you are binding the bottom edge of the skirt rather than hemming it, you'll also need bias tape.

Upholstery zippers. Zippers used for upholstery are typically brass or other metal. Most commonly, you buy the zipper coil by the yard, purchasing the zipper pulls and stops separately. In a pinch, you can purchase standard metal or plastic "sport" zippers instead. Determine the number of individual zipper lengths and total yardage ahead of time.

Batting. Consider adding thin, low-loft batting to the wrong side of a slipcover for extra padding or to improve smoothness and fit.

Tools

The following items are my favorite must-haves for designing and constructing most slipcovers.

Graph paper. Paper with a grid of squares can be useful for plotting your cutting layout and determining the yardage you need.

Marking tools. Dressmaker's chalk or disappearing ink fabric markers are ideal. Choose at least two colors to work with: one color for marking your initial dimensions on the wrong side of the fabric, plus a second color (and a third, if you like) to mark adjustments during fitting.

Fabric shears. When making slipcovers and other large projects, longer blades can make the cutting go faster.

Pinking shears. Pinking the seam allowances is one great way to minimize fabric fraying.

Rotary cutter, mat, and ruler. When cutting large rectangles and squares, a rotary cutting system will save you all kinds of time. Buy a 45 mm or 60 mm cutter and the largest mat and longest ruler you can afford.

Seam ripper. Once the test muslin is fitted, use a seam ripper to deconstruct the pieces, so you can use them as pattern pieces for cutting the slipcover fabric.

Carpenter square (or T-square). This handy tool is great for marking perfectly square corners.

Measuring tape. You'll need an extra-long (120") flexible tape for measuring furniture.

Point turner. For thick and bulky fabrics, a point turner will get the best square corners and the most even curves.

Pins. Longer and sturdier than your average pins, *upholstery pins* can hold heavier-weight fabric without bending out of shape. *T-pins* are fantastic for pinning muslin panels in place on furniture during the fitting process.

Sewing machine needles. Needle sizes 16 and 18 are perfect for heavier upholstery materials. Size 14 can work well for weights such as denim or sateen. Look for *sharp needles* (also called *jeans needles*) rather than universal point needles. Coated needles are best for fabrics with a glaze or finish.

Bobbins. When sewing with heavier upholstery thread, you may find that your sewing machine requires a special bobbin made specifically for this purpose, instead of your standard bobbin. Ask your sewing machine dealer for recommendations.

Presser feet. You may want to invest in a walking foot, Teflon foot, or roller foot to help feed the fabric more evenly through the machine. Also check your sewing machine manual to see if you can adjust the presser-foot pressure on your machine. You'll need a zipper foot for making and attaching piping, welting,

Sewing Machine Tips

Here are a few ways to make the best use of your machine.

- Test swatches of your chosen fabric and thread on your machine before starting your project; make sure your machine can handle them.

- If using upholstery thread, adjust the tension (top and bottom, if possible).

- Make sure fabric pieces are supported as much as possible to take weight off the machine (or to keep the machine from having to pull many pounds of fabric with the feed dogs).

- Use a longer stitch length than usual — 2.5 mm to 3 mm. Of course, use a basting stitch instead when fitting and stitching your muslin.

---

zippers, and other bulky trims. Optional items are piping or cording feet, available in sizes for specific welting diameters.

Jean-a-ma-jig. This gadget is designed to keep the presser foot level; use it behind or in front of the fabric when you begin and end your seam. To make your own, start with a 4" to 6" square scrap of slipcover fabric. Fold it twice to create a 1" to 1½" square with four layers of fabric. Keep folding, if needed, to achieve the appropriate thickness.

Iron and ironing board. Setting and pressing the seams of your finished slipcover will lend them the most professional polish. Pressing is particularly important if making your own bias binding.

CHAPTER TWO

CHOOSING FABRICS

When choosing fabric for a slipcover, consider wearability, cleanability, and comfort. While seldom-used furniture might handle a lighter or more delicate fabric, a daily-used family sofa will need a sturdy fabric that can be cleaned. As a general rule, you want to use woven, medium-weight materials, but there are many types of fibers and fabrics that fall into that category. Also consider potential exposure to sunlight and the likelihood of frequent spots and stains. Are you willing to dry-clean, or do your slipcovers need to be machine washable? Finally, how does the fabric feel against your skin?

CONSIDERATIONS

WHILE THE PRIMARY THINGS TO CONSIDER when selecting slipcover material are fiber and fabric, a few other aspects deserve careful thought as well. The fabric width, print direction, and pattern repeat can have a significant impact on the amount (yardage) of material needed to complete the project. In addition, fabrics of the same fiber and weave can vary in weight, which has its own impact, particularly in sewability and longevity.

Width. Traditionally, upholstery weight fabrics come in 54" to 60" widths. However, some 45"-wide fabrics come in weights suitable for slipcovers, and in delightful prints. While often less expensive per yard, the narrower widths require more yardage, so be aware of how a fabric's width will affect your yardage requirements and overall fabric cost.

Print direction. Another factor that can affect functionality of the fabric, regardless of width, is print direction and repeat. A fabric with a directional print running vertically (parallel to the selvage) needs to be cut on the grain. A fabric with a non-directional print, or a print that runs selvage to selvage, will allow you to *railroad* the fabric. This means that you can cut pieces sideways, on the cross grain of the fabric, which allows fuller use of your yardage, because you can cut even very wide pieces (such as for a sofa back) all in one piece.

A fabric design with a large *repeat* (or other design motif) can lend its own challenges, since you may need to be pickier about positioning the fabric on your furniture (to center a large

**CUTTING
ON GRAIN**

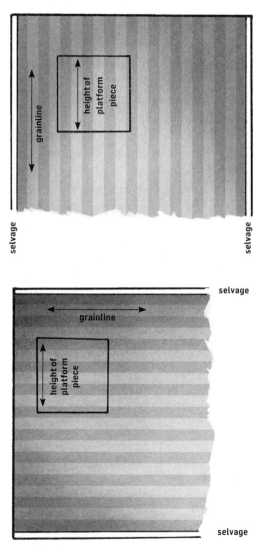

grainline

height of
platform
piece

selvage

selvage

**RAILROADED
PLACEMENT**

selvage

grainline

height of
platform
piece

selvage

motif, for instance). Matching a repeat when piecing a fabric pattern piece or seaming two parts will also require extra yardage.

We'll talk more about how railroading, directional prints, and print repeats can affect your yardage requirements and cutting layouts (see chapter 7, page 82), but it's worth mentioning it now. You'll want to be thinking about such factors when you make an initial visit (or two!) to your local fabric store.

Fabric weight. Lightweight and very heavyweight fabrics are best avoided for slipcovers. Lightweight fabrics simply won't stand up to the wear and tear of sitting and using the furniture, while at the other extreme, a standard sewing machine may have a difficult time sewing through multiple layers of a heavy fabric. When in doubt, buy a swatch and experiment with sewing through at least four layers of the fabric with your machine.

FIBERS

FIBER REFERS SPECIFICALLY TO the raw material of the fabric — plant-based, animal-based, or man-made. I'll start with the most common and popular fibers.

Cotton. Durable, easily laundered, and available in a variety of weaves and weights, cotton is probably the most common natural material available, and the most familiar to today's sewists.

Linen. Made from flax, linen is stronger than cotton, so a lighter-weight linen fabric could be used in place of a heavier cotton fabric. Linen also has a natural sheen, which can be particularly attractive in some settings. It wrinkles easily, but with use, those wrinkles tend to soften into cozy "rumples."

Silk or tussah. Available in a variety of weights and weaves, tussah is raw silk and is usually nubby. While some silk may be laundered, check care instructions carefully — it can develop water spots and fade or deteriorate somewhat quickly. You may need to line silk with muslin, as it can be slippery.

Wool and wool blends. For the purposes of this book, "wool" refers to any fiber made from the fleece of sheep and similar animals. It may be a surprising choice for a slipcover, but one worth considering. Wools provide a certain soft and homey look not available in other fibers. It's strong and durable, while draping nicely. And though it's not usually machine washable, 100 percent pure wool can be dry-cleaned and spot-cleaned. Wool blends may also be worth considering, especially if machine washable. (Always check the care instructions!)

Polyester and poly blends. A poly/cotton blend helps reduce wrinkles, perhaps resulting in a neater finished product, but it can be a little more difficult to shape and handle. Blends are easily laundered, though low-quality goods may not wear well.

Rayon. Rayon is a fiber manufactured from cellulose. It can be quite slippery and not particularly durable, but blended with cotton or linen, it can be a fine choice. Note care and cleaning instructions, since rayons often should be dry-cleaned.

Jute or hemp. Both jute and hemp are very strong plant-based fibers that can stand up to a lot of use. Often, fabrics made from jute and hemp have looser weaves like burlap, which isn't advisable for a slipcover as it can stretch out of shape. However, hemp in particular is now being produced in a variety of comfortable and appropriate weaves.

FABRICS

NOT TO BE CONFUSED WITH FIBER, *fabric* refers to how fibers are woven or knit together to create a particular type and weight of fabric; it's sometimes called a *substrate*. This section discusses the different weaves, finishes, and weights of fabric you might find.

Muslin. While muslin certainly isn't an appropriate fabric for a slipcover, you will use muslin to draft the pattern pieces and finalize fit before cutting and stitching the slipcover fabric. When used as a patterning and designing agent, muslin's fiber, weight, and pattern are unimportant. You may also use muslin as a lining to provide additional strength, structure, and stability to a slippery or less durable outer fabric. It is inexpensive and comes in very narrow (36") and in very wide widths (as much as 108" or even 120"). Alternatively, consider using old bedsheets instead of muslin for the testing and fitting.

Canvas. Canvas may be made from cotton, linen, hemp, or other natural materials. The term refers to heavy, tightly woven fabric. It can come in many different weights and prints.

Denim. Denim is now available in a plethora of colors, prints, and yarn-dyed designs, and in a variety of weights. It's sturdy, and its twill-weave construction often drapes better than a canvas of a similar weight.

Sateen. Sateen tends to be heavier than quilter's cotton, but not quite heavy-duty enough for an upholstery project — in other words, it's *perfect* for slipcovers! Sateen has a slight sheen, and the weight and weave of the fabric give a lovely drape.

Jacquard. This term refers to any fabric woven with a Jacquard loom and includes brocades and damasks. They may be made out of silk, rayon, or synthetic fibers. Brocades may have an embossed surface, while damasks are usually reversible, with the reverse side a mirror image of the front. In any case, in jacquards the background and the foreground design each have different weaves. For instance, the background might have a plain weave, while the patterned area has a satin or twill weave. Light reflects differently on the different weaves, lending visual interest.

Pile fabrics. Pile fabrics — such as velvet and velveteen, corduroy, and chenille — are woven with extra fibers to create a *pile* (cut or uncut loops) on one or both sides of the fabric. They can be made out of natural or man-made fibers. Velveteen and corduroy are typically made from cotton, while velvet usually has a backing of silk or other natural fiber, with a rayon/synthetic pile. Corduroy and chenille have wales, or ribs, of pile, with the plain-weave backing showing between the wales. While a slipcover made from a pile fabric can be very comfy and cozy, there may be care and wear issues. Worn spots, for instance, may be much more visible on a pile fabric than on a plain woven. Some may require dry-cleaning or may spot easily. Look for nonstretch versions of these fabrics if you go this route, so the slipcover doesn't stretch out of shape. Since light reflects differently if the pile is facing different directions, it's also important to cut all pattern pieces for a slipcover made from a pile fabric in the same direction.

Laminated fabrics. Although not the most comfortable to sit or lounge on, these might be just the ticket to create a wipeable, easy-clean covering for surfaces frequented by messy pets and kids.

Outdoor fabrics. Outdoor fabrics resist staining and fading from sunlight. They don't hold creases, which may be a disadvantage if you want crisp pleats. They also tend to be slippery. On the other hand, they're an obvious choice to make slipcovers for outdoor furniture and can be particularly good for pieces with frequent kid or pet usage.

Knit fabrics. While comfy, knit fabrics (including fleece) will quickly stretch out of shape and aren't suitable for a slipcover.

Quilting cottons. Quilting fabrics just aren't sturdy enough to take a lot of wear and tear, so I can't recommend them for slipcovers. However, I, too, have succumbed to the allure of a great print and have tried it for lesser-used furniture pieces: throw pillows, folding-chair covers, cabinet cover-ups, and dining chairs. You can strengthen the fabric with an interfacing or a muslin lining. Do be aware you'll replace covers made with quilting cottons sooner than those made with more durable fabrics, but if you love changing the look of your home frequently, this may not be a concern.

CHAPTER THREE

TRIMS

In this chapter, you'll learn how to make your own welting, which enables you to match or add contrast to the main fabric. We'll also discuss other trims and ideas for including them in your finished projects. Trims help strengthen seams and guard against excessive wear and tear at the corners and edges of your pieces. Since trim is raised, it is the part that will be touched, pressed on, and rubbed against at those seams. Trim can also help hide or distract from any stitching errors, mismatched repeats, and other issues.

THE BASICS

Flanged cord, fringe, and welting are the main types of trims used in slipcovers. While they provide a decorative touch — a little extra splash of color and detail that adds a professional polish — they're also functional, in that they bear the brunt of wear and tear at the seams during daily use.

Flanged cord (sometimes called *lip cord*) is a twisted or braided cord attached to a *flange* (flat strip of fabric). The flange is sewn into the slipcover seam. Flanged cord is available in many different hues; in fact, each *ply*, or strand, of the cord may be a different color.

Upholstery fringe is similarly attached to a flange for sewing into a seam. Throw pillows and slipcover skirt hems are great uses for upholstery fringe.

Welting is to upholstery as piping is to clothing; it consists of a cord encased in fabric. The fabric wrapping includes a flange to sew into the seams of the slipcover or upholstery. Of course, commercially made welting is available at almost any full-service upholstery and home-decor supplies shop, but it is

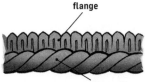

FLANGED CORD

FRINGE

actually very easy to make your own, believe it or not! Trust me, anyone willing to tackle a slipcover project can handle welting!

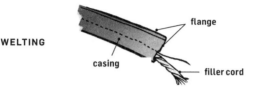

WELTING flange

casing

filler cord

You may choose to make or buy contrast welting, or to *self-welt* the piece, which means creating the welting out of the same fabric used for the slipcover. If your slipcover fabric is particularly heavy, you'll likely want to use a lighter fabric for the trim, to cut down on bulk.

MAKE YOUR OWN WELTING

THE INGREDIENTS FOR DIY WELTING are cable cording or filler cord, plus fabric bias strips to wrap around the cording.

Cable cording is similar to flange cord, minus the flange. Other than taping or stitching the ends to prevent fraying, it requires little special handling. Prewash cotton cording to pre-shrink it.

Filler cord consists of loose cotton stuffed into a mesh tube. Filler cord can fall apart or bunch up when laundered. Plan to dry-clean any slipcovers containing filler cord.

Cording comes in a variety of sizes and may be measured in ¹⁄₁₆" or ¹⁄₃₂" increments. For our purposes, we'll focus on standard sizes: ⅛", ¼", ⅜", and ½" diameters. The casing fabric needs to be wide enough to wrap around the cording plus allow a ½" flange on each raw edge.

Determine the width of the casing's bias strips by adding 1" for the flange (½" at each edge) to the circumference of the cording. For best results, wrap your fabric tightly around the cording to measure. Or use the table below to find the appropriate casing width for a few standard cord sizes, rounded up to the nearest ¼", to give a little extra room for fitting and stitching.

Cut the casing fabric strips on the fabric bias to take advantage of the natural stretch of the bias grain. This will help the welting ease around corners, curves, and other tricky areas. To calculate the yardage of finished welting needed for your slipcover, measure the length of each seam that you wish to welt, add them together, and add an extra 10 percent to the total to allow for ease and seam allowances.

Cutting Bias Strips for Cording

CORDING DIAMETER	CORDING CIRCUMFERENCE	SEAM ALLOWANCE	CUT WIDTH OF BIAS CASING (NUMBERS ROUNDED UP)
⅛"	.39" (.125 × 3.14)	+ 1"	1½"
¼"	.79" (.25 × 3.14)	+ 1"	2"
⅜"	1.18" (.375 × 3.14)	+ 1"	2¼"
½"	1.57" (.5 × 3.14)	+ 1"	2¾"

Figuring Out Welting Yardage

If you're making your own welting, you need to know how many yards of casing you can get out of a given cut of fabric. To help you determine the fabric yardage required for the amount of welting you need, see the chart on page 20 for estimates based on the cut width of the bias strips and the width of a ½ yard of fabric. Remember, all yardages are approximate and may vary.

Cutting Strips from ½ Yard

BIAS STRIP WIDTH	60" FABRIC (YIELD IN YARDS)	54" FABRIC (YIELD IN YARDS)	45" FABRIC (YIELD IN YARDS)
1½"	20–22	16–20	13
1¾"	15–18	14–15	12
2"	12–14	10–12	10
2¼"	10–12	9–11	9
2½"	9–11	8–10	8

MAKING BIAS STRIPS

To make bias strips for a casing, start by trimming away the fabric selvages. Trim the top and bottom cut edges if needed to make the piece perfectly rectangular.

To find the fabric bias, place fabric on your work surface, wrong side up. Fold one trimmed selvage edge down to meet the bottom edge and press. Unfold the fabric. This crease runs along the true bias of the fabric, which is at a 45-degree angle to the selvage and crossgrain. You can then choose the method of cutting and piecing bias strips that you prefer; I'll explain two popular methods here.

FINDING THE BIAS

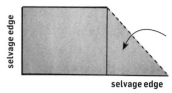

selvage edge

selvage edge

FOLD THIS SELVAGE EDGE
to adjacent raw edge and press along the fold.

Method 1: Strip Piecing

This popular method allows you to piece your strips one by one, interspersing shorter strips with longer strips and discarding very short lengths, to avoid having any two piecing seams too close together. Cutting is faster in this method, but piecing is more time-consuming.

Starting at the pressed bias crease, cut along the bias from the top to bottom edge. You can speed up this process with a rotary cutter, cutting mat, and quilting ruler. Continue cutting parallel to this first cut to create individual bias strips in the determined width (see page 19). Discard any strips less than 4" long. Stitch the strips end to end, right sides facing, with a ¼" seam allowance; offset the angled tips at each short end when stitching so that raw edges meet at the seam. Alternate longer strips with shorter ones throughout the finished casing. Press all seams open and trim seam allowance tips.

Method 2: Continuous Loop

This is my favorite method of making bias strips, although it does have some downsides. In this method, the continuous strip must be cut with scissors, which is more time-consuming. On the other hand, the piecing is much faster, and you will use every square inch of the fabric, which is great for getting the most out of your yardage.

1. Cut the fabric at the pressed bias crease to cut off a 45-degree triangle from one side. Move the triangle to the opposite edge of the fabric, matching trimmed selvages. Using a ¼" seam allowance, stitch selvages together, with right sides facing, to create a parallelogram. Press the seam open.

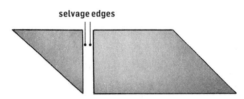

selvage edges

2. Starting at the bias-cut edge of the fabric farthest away from the seam, on the wrong side of the fabric, measure and mark lines parallel to the cut edge and across the width of the fabric in the width determined (see page 19). Once you make the last mark close to the opposite edge, trim off any excess fabric. Mark two more lines, this time across the width of the fabric, parallel to and ¼" in from the top and bottom raw edges. This marks the alignment *and* stitching line for the following steps.

seam line

marked ¼" seam allowance

3. Bring the top and bottom edges of the parallelogram together, right sides facing, to create a tube. At each end

of the tube, line up the raw edge on one side with the first marked line on the other side *at the ¼" seam allowance marking*; offsetting the bias lines like this allows you to cut one long strip in a continuous spiral.

4. Continue lining up the next marked line at one edge with the next marked line at the other edge, pinning as you go, across the width of the fabric, making sure that the marked bias lines at each edge line up at the ¼" seam line. The fabric will seem very twisted and skewed during this process; don't worry — just keep matching and pinning. Once you have pinned at both ends and at all bias markings, stitch at the ¼" seam allowance with a 1 mm stitch length.

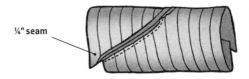

¼" seam

5. Starting at one end of the tube, cut along the bias markings to create the continuous bias strip. Press the seam allowances open.

cutting lines

HOW TO BASTE WELTING TOGETHER

ONCE YOU'VE PIECED AND CUT the bias casing, trim each end to square off. Pile the cording to one side on your sewing table and the pieced bias strip(s) on the other side. This keeps them from getting entangled before assembly. Fold the bias strip in half lengthwise, wrong sides facing, and tuck the cording in between the fabric layers. Let the first 1" to 2" of cording extend past the cut end of the bias casing. Keep the bias strip wrapped tightly around the cording while machine-basting the welting together at a scant ½" seam allowance using a zipper presser foot. Continue until you have sufficient yardage for the project. (To stitch the trim into the seams of the finished slipcover, see Inserting Trims, page 29.)

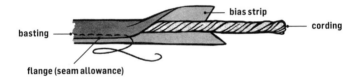

bias strip

cording

basting

flange (seam allowance)

CHAPTER FOUR

SPECIAL TECHNIQUES

This chapter reviews the best tips and tricks for stitching slipcovers and trims. Read on to learn how to handle special sewing challenges for joining pieces of different sizes and shapes, such as easing techniques for slight differences, or darts and tucks for larger variations. Explore different seam-finishing techniques to strengthen seams and minimize fraying. Master the art of inserting zippers, as well as trims such as welting, cording, or fringe. Using these techniques can improve the look and wearability of your slipcovers.

FINESSING SEAMS

SOMETIMES SEAMS NEED a little extra finishing touch. Whether it's strengthening and stabilizing seam allowances, or gently "encouraging" curved edges of different lengths to fit snugly together, here are some options for honing your seaming skills.

Finishing seam allowances. Use pinking shears, a zigzag stitch on your standard sewing machine, or a serger to prevent fraying and to help add stability and strength to the seams of your slipcovers.

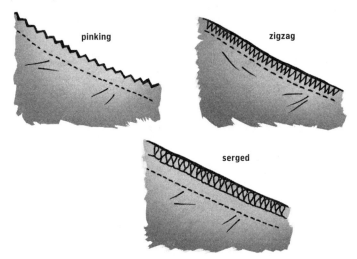

pinking

zigzag

serged

Easing curved areas. If a longer curved edge needs to be eased into a slightly shorter curved or straight edge, baste the larger edge at ¼" and again at ⅜" from the raw edge (assuming a finished seam allowance of ½"; these basting lines should stay completely within your seam allowance); leave long tails at each end. Pull gently on the thread ends on each side of the basting until the larger edge fits the smaller edge. Note that you are not making gathers, but simply drawing in some of the fabric fullness to ease your stitching line around the curved edge.

EASING CURVED AREAS

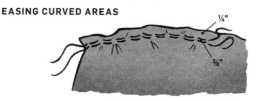

Alternatively, *staystitch* along the curved edge by stitching a straight line through the single layer of fabric at a scant ½" seam allowance (assuming a finished ½" seam allowance). This stitching prevents the fabric from stretching at the curve. Then clip the straight edges and notch the curves to, but not through, the staystitching line, before basting or stitching the pieces together.

SHAPING

THREE-DIMENSIONAL FURNITURE demands a slipcover that is three-dimensional. Sometimes simply stitching a gusset or boxing strip is enough to provide that shape, particularly for a boxy, rectangular piece. More often, the softer, curved lines of your furniture will present an opportunity to sharpen your shaping skills through the use of darts and tucks.

Darts. Use darts in slipcovers much as you would use them in garment sewing: to create a three-dimensional shape in a flat piece of fabric. If the inside back piece is forming the sides and top as well, one common placement of a slipcover dart is at the upper back corners. Darts may be used singly or in groups; the excess fabric is trimmed away (typically cutting out a triangular or square shape in the fabric) before aligning and stitching the adjoining edges of the cutout together.

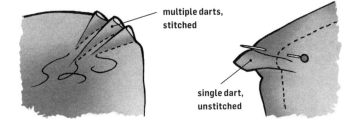

multiple darts, stitched

single dart, unstitched

Tucks. On a curved (not square) corner, add a few small, equally sized and evenly spaced tucks to ease the larger piece into the smaller piece at the corners. Fold and stitch the excess into the seam rather than cutting it away. Tucks look somewhat like miniature pleats, instead of the smoother fit of darts.

tucks

INSERTING TRIMS

TRIMS LEND A PROFESSIONAL POLISH to your slipcover, as well as adding extra strength and resiliency against daily wear and tear. They can be tricky to stitch, however — especially at corners and when joining cut ends of the trim together. Follow these steps to ensure the best results.

Welting

Whenever cutting into a length of cording or welting, adhere masking or Scotch tape around the cord, centered at the cutting point, to keep the ends from fraying. Leave the tape on while stitching.

To install welting into a seam, pin the welting on the right side of one fabric piece, flanged edge aligned to raw edge. If one fabric pattern piece is longer than the other, attach the welting to the larger edge. Baste the welting to the fabric using a zipper foot, starting at least 2" from one cut end. Clip the casing of the welting within the seam allowance as needed to turn corners and ease curves. Pivot at corners and clip. You may also want to *very slightly* bunch, or ease, the welting at corners and curves (see instructions for easing curved areas on page 26) to allow additional ease once the slipcover is turned right side out.

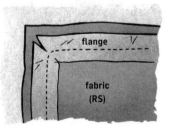

WELTING turning a corner

To join welting ends together, stop stitching 2" before returning to the start. Trim the free end of the welting so that the two ends overlap by at least 1". Remove the basting stitches from the casing and open it to expose the cord at both ends. Finger-press one casing's short raw edge ½" to the wrong side. Tuck the other casing raw edge into the folded edge. The ends will now overlap by ½". Trim the cording so that both ends butt together exactly and tape the ends together to prevent fraying. Finish basting the welting to the fabric, stitching back and forth several times over the join to securely attach it to the fabric.

Place the welted fabric panel on top of the piece you're stitching it to, right sides facing and raw edges aligned; the welting will be sandwiched between the fabric layers. Stitch the fabrics together at a standard ½" seam allowance.

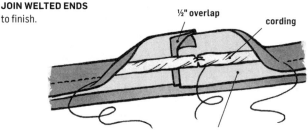

JOIN WELTED ENDS
to finish.

½" overlap

cording

seam allowance wrong side

Flanged Cord

Stitch the flanged cord into slipcover seams as you do with welting; the main difference is in the finishing and joining process.

As with welting, start basting the flanged cord to the fabric at least 2" from the start; tape or use tacky glue on the cord end to keep it from unraveling. If you're joining the ends of the flanged cord, stop stitching 2" before returning to the start of your seam. Trim the free end of the cording so that the two ends overlap by at least 2". Cut 1" of flange away from both cord ends. If one or both ends are taped, remove tape before carefully unwinding both ends just enough to overlap and twist them together. So that the join isn't too bulky, let some of the individual plies angle off into the seam allowance. Once you have the join as neat as you'd like, finish sewing the seam, stitching back and forth several times at the join.

FINISHING FLANGED CORD

Fringe

Inserting fringe into a seam is even easier than welting and flanged cord. The whole process is much the same; however, you usually can't clip into the flange to pivot corners, so ease the corners (see instructions for easing curved areas on page 26) rather than clip and pivot.

When joining the ends, ever so slightly overlap and angle the ends into the seam allowance so that the overlap isn't too bulky and the raw ends aren't exposed when turned inside out. Trim the seam allowances.

ADDING A ZIPPER CLOSURE

The instructions here are for adding a zipper to a slipcover seam. (For details on adding a zipper to a box cushion, see Zippered Seat Cushion or Back Cushion on page 113.) You will need a zipper, or a length of zipper chain plus a zipper pull and stop.

Leave a vertical opening on one side of the slipcover, where the outside back meets the arm. This is where the zipper will be inserted (alternatively, on a larger piece such as a sofa, you may choose to insert the zipper in a centered back seam; the process, however, is the same). The seam allowance on each side of the opening should be a full 1". Measure the open seam from the top of the opening down to the bottom edge of the skirt to determine the length of zipper needed for the project.

Purchase a zipper of this length (or longer), or cut upholstery zipper chain to this length, plus 1". If using a zipper chain, assemble and prep it for use before stitching, as follows:

1. Slide the zipper pull onto one end of the closed chain, and slide it up and down to align the zipper teeth. Attach the zipper stop to the closed end of the zipper.

2. To keep the zipper pull from coming off the open end of the zipper, encase the end of each half of the open zipper tape in a small square of double-fold bias tape or a folded scrap of fabric (great use for any extra casing you might have left over after making welting). Stitch.

With the slipcover removed from the furniture, baste the open vertical seam closed with a 1" seam allowance. Press the seam allowance open. Center the zipper on the wrong side of the basted seam, right side down (wrong sides of zipper and fabric are both facing up toward you). The open end of the zipper should be flush with the hemmed bottom edge of the slipcover.

With a zipper foot, stitch along both sides of the zipper tape and the closed end near the zipper stop. When stitching across the zipper coil, lift your foot off of the pedal and carefully turn your handwheel manually to avoid a broken needle or protesting machine. Flip the zipper panel to the right side and topstitch down the length of the zipper, $3/8$" away from each of the previous stitch lines, to strengthen the seam. Rip the basting stitches out to expose the zipper. (See the illustration on page 115.)

ADDING TIES

FABRIC TIES CAN come in handy to help shape the slipcover, fitting it more snugly on hard-to-fit areas of the furniture. You may know ahead of time that you aren't intending to closely tailor the slipcover, but instead you're planning to use ties to take in the excess fabric; or, you may be faced with the need to install ties after the fact when you realize things don't fit quite as snugly as you wanted. In any case, ties are easy to make and insert into the finished slipcover, either before or after assembly.

Determine the finished length and width of the ties; 1" to 1½" is a typical width. Ties come in pairs, so for each area needing ties, cut two pieces of fabric. Cut each tie 1" longer than the finished length, and 1" wider than *twice* the finished width (for example, 3" wide for a finished width of 1", or 4" wide for a finished width of 1½"). On each tie, fold one short raw edge and both long edges ½" to the wrong side and press. Fold each tie in half lengthwise with wrong sides together and press. Topstitch all three finished edges to secure.

Determine where to insert the ties (for instance, on each side of the front arm piece). If the seams haven't been sewn yet, insert the raw end of each tie into opposite seams and stitch. Make sure the ties are aligned horizontally and vertically, as needed.

If you need to add ties after assembly, use a seam ripper to remove the stitching at the seams, leaving an opening just wide enough to insert the raw end of the tie. Once the tie is inserted, stitch the opening closed, sewing back and forth several times and overlapping your new stitch line with the original seam at least 1" at both ends.

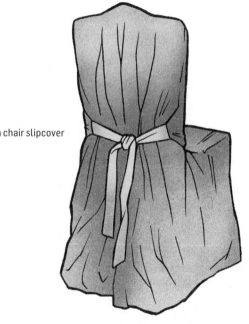

TIES in back of a chair slipcover

ANATOMY OF A SLIPCOVER

Take a peek at this chapter for a crash course in anatomy — the anatomy of a slipcover, that is (no medical degree required)! At the same time, learn how to measure appropriately to get the right fit and determine the necessary yardage. The exact anatomy of a slipcover depends, of course, on the anatomy of the piece it's going to be covering. For your first few slipcover projects, I encourage you to start with furniture pieces primarily constructed of rectangles.

NAMING BODY PARTS

To HELP YOU PLAN YOUR PROJECT, think of the piece you want to cover as a series of planes (flat surfaces). Most often, these planes will be rectangles or squares — the easiest shape to measure, fit, and construct. Occasionally, they may be circles, ovals, trapezoids, or even completely irregular, asymmetrical shapes. These can be more difficult to measure and cut accurately. Some types of furniture that can be easily slipcovered include the following:

- ottomans, which can be rectangular, square, or circular
- backless stools with upholstered seats
- straight chairs with upholstered backs and seats
- armchairs
- loveseats, sofas, and sofa beds

Any furniture type you might consider covering has standard shapes or "body parts." Rather than list them all at once, I'll start with terms common to almost all pieces, from stools to sofas.

Platform (or deck). This is the top surface of an ottoman. The same term is used for the seat of a chair or sofa (or the surface a seat cushion rests on).

Drop (part of the platform). If the fabric of a slipcover's platform wraps over the edge and drops down one or more sides of the furniture (rather than being seamed to a separate piece at the top edge), this is called a *drop*. In construction, it is the part of the platform fabric that overhangs the top edge(s). Of course, you may choose to omit a drop entirely in your slipcover and create a *boxing strip* (see below) to meet the platform at the top edge of your piece.

Boxing strip. Although this part is sometimes referred to as a *side band* or *gusset,* I'll use the term *boxing* in this book. I use *gusset* to refer exclusively to those (optional) pieces forming the sides of a chair or sofa back.

The boxing is formed from a separate fabric strip (or pieced strips), to add a necessary third dimension to your slipcover, while a drop is part of the platform fabric. You need boxing on any side that does not contain a drop. A slipcover could contain both a dropped edge *and* boxing, as well as a skirt; it is up to you how many pieces and parts you want your slipcover to have. Boxing is also used on chair and sofa cushion covers to create a three-dimensional, boxed shape.

Piecing a Boxing Strip

Any time the boxing strip needs to be wider than the fabric width you're using, you will need to piece the boxing together unless you're railroading the fabric (see page 10). (For specific calculation and piecing instructions, see Skirt Piecing and Piecing Allowance, pages 90–92). During the calculation and piecing process, consider the placement of the seams. Do you want them equally spaced all around the ottoman, or at each corner, or does the shape lend itself to a different placement? Measure from the chosen placement of each seam to the next to determine the width of each cut piece, adding a 1" seam allowance to the measurement of each strip for piecing them together.

Skirt. This part of the slipcover can hang from the drop or the boxing strip. The finished length usually measures anywhere from 4" to the full distance to the floor. If you decide to omit a skirt entirely, be sure to add an appropriate hem allowance to the bottom edge of your drop or boxing (whichever piece serves as the bottom edge of the slipcover). Follow the hemming guidelines in Style Your Skirt (see pages 74–77).

··

Room to Maneuver

The measurements on the following pages are *estimates* for the final cut measurements. Use the measuring charts in this chapter to keep track. After you mark the measured dimensions on muslin (for best results, make a test slipcover in muslin before cutting the final fabric), *add a 2" fitting allowance around all edges of each marked piece*. This will allow room for measuring error, and ease for fitting around the furniture frame. While you're fitting, use a fabric marker in a contrasting color to mark the seams. With the contrasting colors, you'll be able to note more easily which marks indicate the correct, updated measurements.

Many slipcover how-to's suggest adding that 2" excess to your initial measurements (*prior* to marking the muslin), but I prefer to add it *outside* my markings as described above. I like having the actual measurements marked first, since I think it allows me to position my fabric pieces more precisely on the furniture while fitting, and it gives me a better idea of how my final seamlines fall in relation to my initial measurements of the furniture parts.

··

OTTOMANS AND STOOLS

OTTOMANS ARE UPHOLSTERED PIECES of furniture that usually have short legs, with the upholstered "body" or frame making up most of the piece. Stools, on the other hand, may be upholstered or not and their legs are typically longer, making up more of the piece's construction. Both are backless and may be either rectangular or round. We'll deal with rectangular and round pieces separately, as the measuring and piecing process differs slightly for each.

Measuring a Rectangular Ottoman

Rectangular ottomans may have a drop on zero, two, or all four sides. The examples on page 42 show one ottoman with boxing and the other with a drop. Approach your measurements as follows.

Platform. Measure the length and width at the widest points. If the piece is irregularly shaped, you can make any necessary adjustments to the pattern when fitting. Add 1" to each measurement for seam allowances.

Drop. If including a drop on the platform, measure from the edge of the platform down to the first seam of the piece, or where you wish the seam to fall if you're not following the shape of the existing upholstery. Add this to each edge where you plan to have a drop, including the 1" seam allowances added above. Be aware that if your fabric is directional and you're planning a drop on all four sides, the fabric print will be upside down on one side and sideways on two more.

Boxing. *If there is no drop,* measure the length from the top edge down to where you want the bottom edge of the boxing to land; add 1" for seam allowances. *If there is a drop,* measure the length from the bottom edge of the drop to the bottom seam of the boxing; add 1" for seam allowances. To determine the full finished width (perimeter) of the boxing, measure across each side that will contain boxing and add these together. Add 1" for seam allowances.

Skirt. Measure the length from the top edge of the skirt (where it will meet the drop or boxing) down to where the skirt will end. At their shortest, finished skirt lengths are usually at least 4" and often stop ¼" or ½" above the floor (skimming but not actually touching the floor). For a standard hem, add 3" to this length. (For other hemming options that may affect the cut length, see Hems on pages 74–81.)

Measure skirt width by measuring around the entire circumference of the piece at its widest point and add 1" for seam allowance. (For information on adding ease, pleat, ruffle, or gathering allowances, see chapter 6, page 64.) After all allowances are taken into consideration for the width, if this final measurement is wider than the width of the fabric you're using, you'll need to piece the skirt (see Skirt Piecing and Piecing Allowance, pages 90–92).

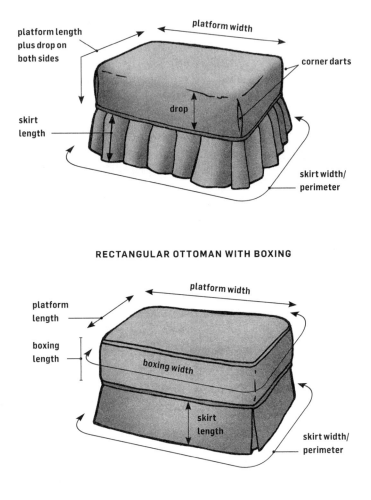

RECTANGULAR OTTOMAN WITH A DROP

platform length plus drop on both sides

platform width

corner darts

drop

skirt length

skirt width/ perimeter

RECTANGULAR OTTOMAN WITH BOXING

platform length

platform width

boxing length

boxing width

skirt length

skirt width/ perimeter

Measuring a Circular Ottoman or Stool

Measure the boxing and skirt on a circular ottoman or stool in the same fashion as for a rectangular ottoman. The only differences will be in the platform and drop measurements. Note that there are fewer drop options in a circular piece, and in fact a drop is less common (and more challenging) in round pieces.

Platform. Measure the diameter of the platform surface at the center (at the platform's widest point). Make any necessary adjustments to an oblong pattern when fitting. Add 1" to the measurement for seam allowances.

Drop. A circular ottoman or stool either has no drop, or a drop all the way around. If you want a drop, note that you will need to take in a lot of fullness on the dropped edge, either with gathers (see pages 72–73) or a series of tucks or darts (see Shaping, page 27). If including a drop on the platform, measure from the top edge of the stool down to the seam, or wherever you wish the new seam to fall if you're not following the shape of the existing upholstery. Double this measurement and add it to the diameter of the platform. Be sure to include the 1" seam allowance added above. Be aware that if your fabric is directional and you're considering a drop, the fabric print will be upside down or sideways around much of the piece.

Boxing and skirt. Follow the instructions starting on page 41.

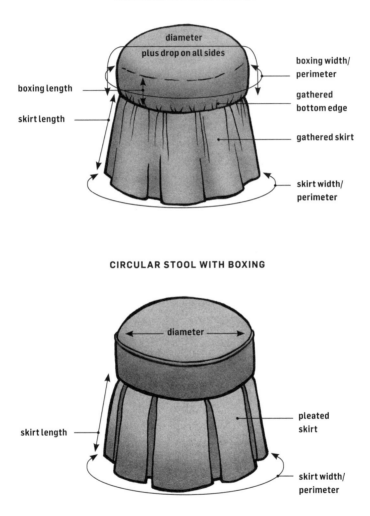

CIRCULAR STOOL WITH DROP

diameter
plus drop on all sides

boxing width/
perimeter

boxing length

gathered
bottom edge

skirt length

gathered skirt

skirt width/
perimeter

CIRCULAR STOOL WITH BOXING

diameter

skirt length

pleated
skirt

skirt width/
perimeter

CIRCULAR STOOL WITH BOXING AND NO SKIRT

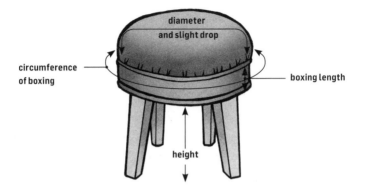

Measuring Chart for Ottoman or Stool (Rectangular or Round)

	LENGTH			WIDTH (PERIMETER FOR BOXING AND SKIRT)		
	MEASURE	ADD'L	TOTAL	MEASURE	ADD'L	TOTAL
Platform*		+ 1"			+ 1"	
Drop (per side)						
Boxing		+ 1"			+ 1"	
Skirt		+ 3"**			***	
Trimmed seams (page 63)		+ 10%				

* If using this chart for a circular ottoman or stool, enter the diameter in the length and width boxes.

** For straight hemmed skirts; for additional options, see Hems (pages 74–77).

*** See chapter 6, Style Your Skirt (pages 64–73), for flat skirt, pleat, and gathering options and allowances.

STRAIGHT CHAIRS WITHOUT ARMS

THE MORE PARTS THERE ARE to a piece of furniture, the more complex the measuring and piecing. We'll now work with an armless (straight) chair, which introduces a back, but omits the arms of an easy chair or sofa.

Platform. Measure the length of the seat from the back edge to the front at the longest point. Measure the width of the seat at the widest point. If the platform is irregularly shaped, make any necessary adjustments to the pattern when fitting. If the chair is fully upholstered, the platform will need a tuck-in allowance at the back edge only (see the box on page 47). Add 1" to each measurement for seam allowances.

Drop. You may have no drop, a front drop only, or drop on the front and both sides. Measure from the edge of the platform down to where you wish the drop to end. Add this length to any side you plan to add a drop to. Be sure to include the 1" seam allowance, originally added to the platform.

Boxing. *Without a drop*, measure the length from the edge of the seat down to the bottom edge of the boxing; add 1" for seam allowances. *With a drop*, measure the length from the drop's bottom edge to the bottom seam of the boxing; add 1" for seam allowances. To determine the finished width of the boxing, measure across each side that will contain boxing and add these together; add 1" for seam allowances.

Inside back. As the name suggests, the inside back is the side of the chair that your back rests on when sitting. In slipcover anatomy, this includes the entire depth of the upper edge of the chair or sofa, and often the entire width of the side edges of the back as well.

....

What Is a Tuck-in Allowance?

A *tuck-in allowance* is fabric that is tucked into the crevices found at certain joints of an upholstered piece. It helps increase the longevity of the piece by reducing stress on the seams at those points. Like the drop mentioned above, the tuck-in allowance is a measurement added to a fabric pattern piece only as needed.

On an upholstered straight chair, such as a Parsons chair, a tuck-in might be found at the seam joining the inside back to the platform. On an armchair or sofa, tuck-ins are used at that same back seam, as well as the seams joining the inside arm to the platform and where the inside arms meet the inside back.

The tuck-in allowance is typically between 2" and 4" on each side of certain seams and may go up to 6" on a plush upholstered piece. Our instructions and measuring charts standardize this to 3"; adjust up or down as you deem necessary. To check the depth of the tuck-in crevices, try inserting a straight ruler between the platform and inside arms and inside back. Regardless, be consistent each time you add the allowance for a slipcover's parts.

....

Measure the length at the longest point, *including the entire depth of the upper back edge.* If you are creating separate back cushion and seat cushion covers, remove the cushions before measuring. On an upholstered piece, the inside back needs a 3" tuck-in allowance added to the bottom edge only. Measure the width at the widest point. Include the entire width of the back sides, unless making separate *back gussets* (see below) (gussets, like the boxing, provide three-dimensional shaping to the slipcover; in this case, to the chair back). If the shape is irregular or curved, make any necessary adjustments to the pattern during the fitting process. Add a 1" seam allowance to each measurement.

Outside back. This piece faces away behind you when you are seated. Measure the length at the longest point, from the top edge down to the point you wish the skirt to attach (if adding a skirt), or down to the point you want the bottom edge of the slipcover to land. If you are extending the boxing to the back, instead measure down to the top edge of the boxing. In any case, add 1" for seam allowances. Measure the width at the widest point. If the shape is irregular or curved, make any necessary adjustments to the pattern during the fitting process. Add 1" for seam allowances.

Back gusset. The back gussets cover the sides of the chair or sofa back. They're only needed if the shape of the furniture dictates it, or if you simply prefer not to wrap the inside back piece around and over the sides. On a straight chair, the length extends from the top edge of the back, down to the point the back meets the seat, or perhaps even to the bottom edge of the seat, depending on overall shaping.

Measure the length at the longest point, starting at the top edge and continuing down to where the back meets the seat (or down to the bottom edge of the seat, if needed). If the shape is irregular, make any necessary adjustments to the pattern during the fitting process. Add 1" for seam allowances. Measure the

Measuring Chart for a Straight Chair without Arms

	LENGTH (INCLUDES TUCK-IN)			WIDTH		
	MEASURE	ADD'L	TOTAL	MEASURE	ADD'L	TOTAL
Platform		+ 4"*			+ 1"	
Drop (per side)						
Boxing		+ 1"			+ 1"	
Inside back		+ 4"*			+ 1"	
Outside back		+ 1"			+ 1"	
Back gussets (2)		+ 1"			+ 1"	
Skirt		+ 3"**			**	
Trimmed seams (page 63)		+ 10%				

* Includes tuck-in for upholstered pieces. Subtract 3" if seat and back are not upholstered.

** See chapter 6, Style Your Skirt (pages 64–73), for flat skirt, pleat, and gathering options and allowances.

width at the widest point. If the shape is irregular or curved, make any necessary adjustments to the pattern during the fitting process. Add 1" for seam allowances.

Skirt. Measure the perimeter (width) of the skirt as for an ottoman (see page 41).

STRAIGHT CHAIR WITH A FRONT DROP AND BOXING AT THE SIDES

back width (at widest point)

back gusset width

inside back length

back gusset length

outside back length

platform length

platform width

boxing length

skirt width

boxing width

front drop length

skirt length

ARMCHAIRS AND SOFAS

YES, ADDING ARMS to the equation presents a somewhat tougher challenge than the previous projects, but you can do it! For larger pieces, it never hurts to measure in a few places, to make sure you are taking the largest measurement for any given part. But no matter what, you'll be testing the fit before you stitch, so don't fret.

Platform. If you prefer to have your slipcover go right over your seat and back cushions, take all measurements with the cushions left in place. Then the top of the cushions becomes the platform. This makes for a simpler slipcover. If you are creating separate back and seat cushion covers, remove the cushions before measuring. Measure the length from the back of the platform to the front at the longest point.

If the platform extends beyond and in front of the arms (forming a T or L shape) or is otherwise irregularly shaped, measure the width at the widest point. Make any necessary adjustments to the pattern when fitting. On an upholstered piece, the platform will need a tuck-in allowance (see What is a Tuck-in Allowance?, page 47) at the back edge and both sides. Add 1" to each measurement for seam allowances.

Drop. A drop on an armchair or sofa is found only on the front of the piece, and only to eliminate a seam at the front of the platform. Measure from the edge of the platform down to where you wish the drop to end. Add this length to the front edge of the platform. Be sure to include the seam allowance originally added to the platform.

Boxing. Measure the length from the front edge of the platform (or the bottom edge of the drop, if one exists) to the point the skirt is attached; add 1" for seam allowances. Measure the width across the front of the chair or sofa at the widest point, adding 1" for seam allowance. If you want to extend the boxing strip to wrap around the sides and/or back, measure the width of those areas as well.

Inside back. As the name suggests, the inside back is the side of the chair that your back rests on when sitting. In slipcover anatomy, this includes the entire depth of the upper edge of the chair or sofa, and often the entire width of the side edges of the back as well.

Measure the length at the longest point, *including the entire depth of the upper back edge.* If you are creating separate back cushion and seat cushion covers, remove the cushions before measuring. On an upholstered piece, the inside back needs a 3" tuck-in allowance added to the bottom edge only. Measure the width at the widest point. Include the entire width of the back sides, unless making separate *back gussets* (see page 53) (gussets, like the boxing, provide three-dimensional shaping to the slipcover; in this case, to the chair back). If the shape is irregular or curved, make any necessary adjustments to the pattern during the fitting process. Add a 1" seam allowance to each measurement.

Outside back. This piece faces away behind you when you are seated. Measure the length at the longest point, from the top edge down to the point you wish the skirt to attach (if adding a skirt), or down to the point you want the bottom edge of the slipcover to land. If you are extending the boxing to the back, instead measure down to the top edge of the boxing. In any case, add 1" for seam allowances. Measure the width at the widest point. If the shape is irregular or curved, make any necessary adjustments to the pattern during the fitting process. Add 1" for seam allowances.

Back gusset. In an armchair or sofa, the length would typically extend from the top edge of the back down to the top of the arm. Measure the length at the longest point, starting at the top edge, down to the top of the arm (depending on furniture construction, the back gusset may have another logical bottom edge; let your individual piece be your guide). Add 1" for seam allowances. Measure the width at the widest point. If the shape is irregular or curved, make any necessary adjustments to the pattern during the fitting process. Add 1" for seam allowances.

Inside arm. This part of the sofa arm faces toward you when sitting. In slipcover anatomy, the length usually includes the entire depth of the upper edge of the arm and, occasionally, a small drop over to the outside arm. The length and width may also extend somewhat over and onto the front arm, depending on construction.

Measure the length of the inside arm at the longest point, typically including the full depth of the top arm, up and over to wherever you want the seam to fall (where this piece meets the outside arm). Add 3" for a tuck-in allowance to the bottom edge (see What is a Tuck-in Allowance?, page 47), and a 1" seam allowance. Measure the width of the inside arm at the longest point — this may include some portion of the front of the arm, and it should also extend all the way to the very back edge of the arm. Add 3" for a tuck-in allowance to the back edge and 1" for seam allowances.

Top arm. Typically, the top edge of the arm is included as part of the inside arm fabric piece, particularly if the arm has a curved inside edge; however, this isn't always the case, particularly if the arm is comprised of completely square edges. Let the construction of the furniture be your guide in deciding whether or not your slipcover warrants a separate top arm piece. If creating a separate top arm pattern, measure length and width at the longest and widest points. Add a 1" seam allowance to each measurement (see table on page 57).

Outside arm. This side of the arm faces away from you when sitting. Typically the top seam of the outside arm fabric falls a bit below the arm's actual topmost edge. To determine the top and bottom seams, you may want to use your couch's existing seams as a guide (though you can choose different points at which to place your seams).

Measure the length at the longest point, from the top seam down to where you will attach the skirt. If you are extending the boxing to the sides, you will instead measure down to the top seam of the boxing. Add 1" for seam allowances. Measure the outside arm's width at the widest part. If the shape is irregular, make any necessary adjustments to the pattern during the fitting process. Add 1" for seam allowances.

Front arm. This side of the arm faces forward and away from the back. For anything other than a rectangular shape, be sure to measure the front arm at the widest and longest points.

Make any necessary adjustments to the pattern during fitting. If the inside and outside arm pieces fold over to the front on the original piece and you want to keep this detail in your slipcover, measure from seam to seam for length and width. Add a 1" seam allowance to each measurement.

Back arm. This piece only exists if the arms fall outside the boundaries of the chair/sofa back. For anything other than a rectangular shape, be sure to measure the back arm at the widest and longest points. Make any necessary adjustments to the pattern during fitting. Add a 1" seam allowance to each measurement.

Skirt. Measure the perimeter (width) of the skirt as for an ottoman (see page 41).

ARMCHAIR

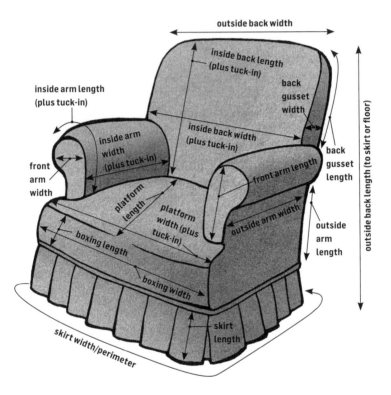

outside back width

inside back length
(plus tuck-in)

back gusset width

inside arm length
(plus tuck-in)

inside arm width
(plus tuck-in)

inside back width
(plus tuck-in)

front arm width

back gusset length

platform length

front arm length

platform width (plus tuck-in)

outside arm width

boxing length

outside arm length

outside back length (to skirt or floor)

boxing width

skirt width/perimeter

skirt length

Measuring Chart for an Armchair or Sofa

Some of these pieces may not be needed in the slipcover for your particular piece; let the furniture's anatomy be your guide.

	LENGTH			WIDTH		
	MEASURE	ADD'L	TOTAL	MEASURE	ADD'L	TOTAL
Platform		+ 4"*			+ 7"*	
Drop (front)						
Boxing		+ 1"			+ 1"	
Inside back		+ 4"*			+ 1"	
Outside back		+ 1"			+ 1"	
Inside arm		+ 4"*			+ 4"*	
Top arm		+ 1"			+ 1"	
Outside arm		+ 1"			+ 1"	
Front arm		+ 1"			+ 1"	
Back arm		+ 1"			+ 1"	
Skirt		+ 3"**			**	
Trimmed seams (page 63)		+ 10%				

* Includes tuck-in for upholstered pieces; subtract 3" if seat, back, and/or arms are not upholstered.

** See chapter 6, Style Your Skirt (pages 64–73), for flat skirt, pleat, and gathering options and allowances.

CUSHIONS

CREATING NEW COVERS FOR SEAT and back cushions is an important part of slipcovering an upholstered armchair or sofa, unless you design the slipcover to go over the cushions as well as the frame. In that case, you can safely ignore this section; but be sure to measure all parts of your furniture with the cushions in place, and allow for a little extra tuck-in allowance. Here we'll cover the process for seat and back *box* cushions, both rectangular and T- or L-shaped. We will not cover knife-edged cushions in this book, which consist only of two main panels (no boxing).

Measuring Seat Cushions

Each seat cushion typically consists of top and bottom panels, a zipper panel at the back, and boxing at the front and sides. On a sofa, each seat cushion may have a unique shape and size; be sure to measure all cushions individually to verify you have correct sizes noted for each.

Top and bottom panels. Two panels are required for each seat cushion: top and bottom. Note that if a cushion is asymmetrical (L-shaped, for instance), front and back panels must be reversed when marked and cut. If you have more than one cushion to cover, make sure you keep track of how many total panels you need in each dimension, and whether any need to be reversed, before you start tackling yardage requirements and cutting layouts. Once you start cutting, label each pattern accordingly.

Measure the length and width of each seat cushion at the largest points. If any cushion is T-shaped, L-shaped, or trapezoidal, sketch out the dimensions on a sheet of graph paper before marking, or simply place the cushion on muslin and trace around it. Cushions that are L- or T-shaped have one or two *ears*, respectively (the parts that stick past the main cushion body), the depth of which should be measured separately. Add 1" to each measurement for seam allowances.

Zipper panel. To determine height, measure the height of the cushion and add 2". To determine cut panel width, measure the cushion's current zipper and add 2". The zipper and panel should wrap around the back corners of the cushion by at least 3" on each side to make it easier to insert the cushion into the finished cover.

Boxing. Measure the height of the cushion and add 1". To find the cut width, measure the cushion perimeter, minus the back zipper panel — from one side, across the front, and then the other side. Add 4" to this measurement. If this measurement exceeds the width of the fabric, you will need to piece the boxing from multiple panels (see Panel Piecing Tips, pages 89–91).

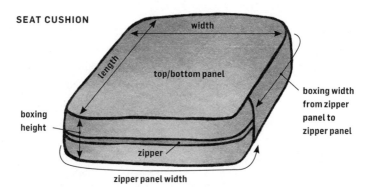

SEAT CUSHION

width

length

top/bottom panel

boxing width from zipper panel to zipper panel

boxing height

zipper

zipper panel width

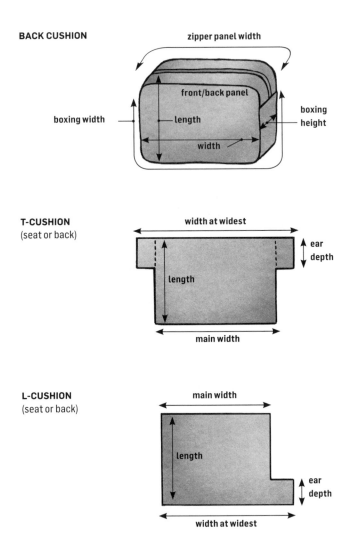

BACK CUSHION

zipper panel width

front/back panel

boxing width

length

boxing height

width

T-CUSHION
(seat or back)

width at widest

ear depth

length

main width

L-CUSHION
(seat or back)

main width

length

ear depth

width at widest

Measuring Back Cushions

Each back cushion typically consists of a front and back panel, a zipper panel, and boxing around the top and sides. On a sofa, each cushion may have a unique shape and size; measure all cushions to make sure you have noted the correct sizes for each.

Front and back panels. Two panels are required for each cushion: front and back. Note that if a cushion is asymmetrical (L-shaped, for instance), front and back panels must be reversed when marked and cut. If you have more than one cushion to cover, make sure you keep track of how many total panels you need, in each dimension, and whether any need to be reversed, before you start tackling yardage requirements and cutting layouts. Once you start cutting, label each pattern accordingly.

Measure the length and width of each cushion at the largest points. If any cushion is T-shaped, L-shaped, or trapezoidal, sketch out the dimensions on a sheet of graph paper before marking — or simply place the cushion on muslin and trace around it. Cushions that are L- or T-shaped have one or two *ears*, respectively (the parts that stick past the main cushion body), the depth of which should be measured separately. Add 1" to each measurement for seam allowances.

Zipper panel. To determine height, measure the height of the cushion and add 2". To find the cut panel width, measure the cushion's current zipper and add 2". The zipper and panel should wrap around the bottom corners of the cushion by at least 3" on each side to make it easier to insert the cushion into the finished cover.

Boxing. Measure the height of the cushion and add 1". To find the finished cut *width*, measure the remainder of the cushion perimeter, minus the bottom zipper panel (up one side, across the top, and down the other side). Add 4" to this measurement. If this measurement exceeds the width of the fabric, you will need to piece the boxing from multiple panels (see Panel Piecing Tips, pages 89–91).

Measuring Chart for Seat and Back Cushions

	LENGTH			WIDTH		
	MEASURE	ADD'L	TOTAL	MEASURE	ADD'L	TOTAL
Main panels (2)		+ 1"			+ 1"	
Zipper panel		+ 2"			+ 2"	
Boxing		+ 1"			+ 4"	
L- or T-shaped ears		+ 1			+ 1"	
Trimmed seams (page 63)		+ 10%				

Seams with Trim

As a last step to all measuring charts, take a look at your furniture piece and measure all seams that you plan to add trim to, whether it's welting, cording, or fringe. Examples include around the front arm piece, at the top of the skirt, at the top edge of the boxing strip, around the outside back, around the outside arm — and don't forget the seat cushions! Add all these measurements together to determine the total finished length of trim needed; add at least another 10 percent to this length to find the total yardage of trim you'll need to start with. (See Make Your Own Welting, pages 18–24, for more on creating your own trim, and Inserting Trims, pages 29–32, for tips on stitching them into the slipcover.)

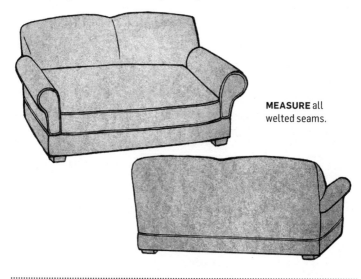

MEASURE all welted seams.

CHAPTER SIX

STYLE YOUR SKIRT

No home-decor look is complete without considering pleats, gathers, or other design elements that can improve the fit as well as the look of your slipcover. In this chapter, you'll learn the difference between box pleats, inverted pleats, knife pleats, gathers, and more. Pleats and gathers, in particular, can affect the yardage requirements and cutting dimensions of the slipcover skirt, so we'll consider all those options next. Where is the best location to place these elements? How much extra fabric will you need? All of these questions — and more — will be answered, no fear.

The cut *length* of your skirt can vary somewhat depending on the type of hem you choose. However, the required starting *width* of the skirt is a much more dynamic variable. To determine the starting width, you need to consider carefully whether you want a flat tailored skirt, gathers, or pleats, and, if the latter, how many. The choices you make between a tailored skirt, corner pleats or gathers, or allover pleats or gathers (as well as the type of pleat: knife, inverted, or box) can significantly impact the starting width of the skirt and, therefore, the amount of fabric and number of panels you need to complete your skirt.

This chapter will show you how to calculate what you need to add to your skirt's finished perimeter to achieve the finished style you want. Use Calculating Your Skirt Measurements, on page 74, to keep track of your measurements.

Once you've constructed and hemmed the skirt following the instructions in this chapter, stitch it to the bottom of the slipcover body as follows.

Without zipper closure. Stitch the short ends of the slipcover to form a ring. Place slipcover and skirt together, right sides facing, aligning raw edges. Adjust to position any pleats, gathers, and seams as desired. Stitch together with ½" seam allowance.

With zipper closure. Place slipcover and skirt together, right sides facing, aligning raw edges. Ensure that the zipper openings on each piece match up. Stitch together with ½" seam allowance at long raw edge only, leaving zipper seam open.

FLAT SKIRTS

A FLAT SKIRT IS SIMPLY ONE WITHOUT gathers or pleats. Even if you don't want any extra flair in the skirt, you still need to allow for more width in your finished skirt than the actual circumference or perimeter of the furniture. This extra ease allows it to hang smoothly, particularly on larger chairs and sofas. Just as your clothes usually need ease to move and wrap easily around your body, so does a slipcover skirt! Allow for *at least* 1" of ease around each corner.

FLAT SKIRT WITH STRAIGHT HEMS

PLEATS

PLEATS ARE CREASED FOLDS in your fabric. They come in a variety of configurations, from the very basic single knife pleat to a more complex inverted or box pleat. In a slipcover's skirt, they are typically located either at the corners or evenly spaced all around. In this section, I'll describe how to make each type and provide the total pleat allowance needed for each style. In addition to pleat allowance, other allowances that impact the full skirt width include closure and piecing allowances (see Additional Allowances, page 73).

Corner box pleats or inverted box pleats. These double-fold pleats are simply mirror images of each other, so they require the same fabric allowance. Inverted pleats are more common when used only at the corners. You can make pleats in a variety of widths, but for the sake of simplicity, instructions here are for 6" pleats. Add or subtract from that number as desired.

FINISHED BOX PLEAT

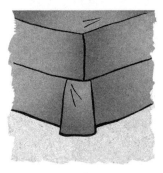

FINISHED INVERTED BOX PLEAT

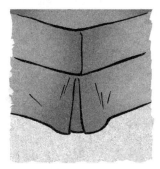

Measuring for Box Pleats

Whether you want box or inverted pleats, the measuring process is the same. Start by making a mark (A, page 68) at the center of the pleat; for finished placement, this would be at the corner of the skirt in most cases. Make this mark on the *wrong* side of the fabric for a box pleat, or on the *right* side of the fabric for an inverted pleat, but always *mark within seam allowances* so they don't show on the finished slipcover. Make two more marks (B) at 6" from both sides of the center mark. Fold the fabric (as shown on page 68 for the pleat of your choice) so that the B marks meet at point A (the center). Baste to secure.

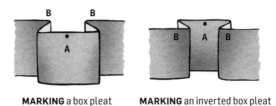

MARKING a box pleat   **MARKING** an inverted box pleat

When you're ready to make the box pleat for the next corner, remember that the right- and left-hand B marks meet at (and form) the corner, for corner pleats; the 12" space between them (with the mark A in the center) is the excess fabric that forms the pleat. Thus, when marking the pleats for the next corner(s), make the closest mark B where the next corner will fall; then make mark A 6" farther away, and the second mark B another 6" farther.

To figure your total yardage for pleats, each 6"-wide box or inverted pleat requires a 12" pleat allowance. Thus, for four corner pleats, add 48" (12" per corner) for the pleat allowance.

Corner knife pleats. A knife pleat is a single-fold pleat. It can point right or left. If you are placing the pleats at the corners only, you may wish to have the two front corner pleats point *away* from the front center in opposite directions, and ditto for the two back corner pleats. While you can make knife pleats in any width, these instructions are for 3" pleats. Adjust that width as you like.

left side   **right side**

FINISHED
CORNER KNIFE
PLEAT

Measuring for Knife Pleats

To make a 3" knife pleat, mark A on the right side of the fabric (for finished placement, this would be at the corner of the skirt). Mark B at 6" to the right *or* left of A (6" to the left for a right-facing pleat; 6" to the right for a left-facing pleat). Fold to move mark B to mark A. The excess fabric folds to the wrong side of the fabric.

When you're ready to make the knife pleat for the next corner, remember that the A and B marks meet at (and form) the corner; the 6" space between them is excess. Thus, make the first mark where the corner is in relation to the previous corner, and make a second mark 6" farther away. Which mark is A and which is B will depend on whether you're making a right- or left-facing pleat.

To figure your total, assuming a 3"-deep knife pleat, each individual pleat requires an additional 6" pleat allowance. For four corner knife pleats, then, add 24" (6" per corner) for the pleat allowance.

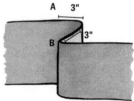

MARKING a knife pleat

Allover knife pleats. These are plotted and marked the same way as corner knife pleats. Assuming a 3"-deep pleat, each individual pleat requires an additional 6" pleat allowance. Determine the number of pleats to make, multiply by 6", and add this total for the pleat allowance.

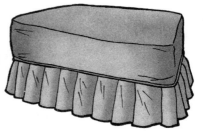

ALLOVER KNIFE PLEATS

GATHERS

WHILE PLEATS LEND a sharp, tailored look to your slipcover, gathers create a soft, warm feel, reminiscent of cozy nights snuggled up with a good book and a cup of tea.

Making Corner Gathers

Gathered corners offer a softer alternative to corner pleats, without the fussier look of full-fledged ruffles. The following calculations are based on corner gathers that span a total of 6" around each corner (3" on each side.) The fabric in a gathered area is usually twice the final width, so start with 6" extra fabric at each corner. Find and mark the center of this 12" span, which is where you want the corner to fall. Make two additional marks at 6" on each side of the center.

Baste two stitch lines within the seam allowance (one at ¼" and one at ⅜" from the raw edge) between the two outer marks. Leave the thread tails long. Pull the threads gently until the fabric is gathered evenly and measures 6" between the two outer marks (see the illustration for easing curved areas, page 27).

To figure your total, assuming corner gathers that extend 3" on each side of the corner, each corner requires a 6" gathering allowance. For four corner gathers, then, add 24" (6" per corner) for the pleat allowance.

FINISHED GATHERED CORNER

Making Allover Gathers

You can also fully gather the skirt of your slipcover for a more dressy style. It's an easy allowance to calculate: start with twice the finished width. It's also forgiving, in the event your math is ever so slightly off, because a slightly smaller or larger allowance is easily accommodated in the gathering process.

For large gathered areas, I suggest gathering in sections using the dental floss + zigzag stitch method; upholstery thread, hand-quilting thread, or another strong thread or yarn can be substituted for floss. First, measure to find the distance between each of the four corners on your furniture. Double each of these side measurements, and mark these doubled amounts on the skirt fabric. Cut four pieces of dental floss that are at least 12" longer than each marked section. Starting at one corner mark on the skirt and stopping at the next, hold the floss against the fabric and zigzag stitch within the seam allowance. Let the zigzag stitches *pass over* the floss without piercing it. Leave at least 6" of floss at each end of the stitch line and secure the ends by tying them around a pin.

Repeat for each side.

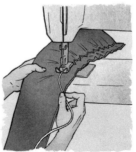

USE FLOSS and a zigzag stitch to make gathers.

Pull the floss to gather the fabric on each side, until you reach the correct width. Pin and baste the gathered fabric with an edgestitch to secure. If adding a zipper closure, leave at least 1" ungathered at each end.

FINISHED ALLOVER GATHERS

Additional Allowances

Closure allowances. For a very snug-fitting slipcover, or for a larger slipcover (as on a sofa), you may wish to add a zipper closure to one of the slipcover's vertical back seams. Such a zipper extends into the skirt and requires an additional allowance. If planning to add a zipper to the slipcover, add 2" to the calculated skirt width for a zipper closure allowance and seam allowances. If not, only add 1" for the seam allowances.

Piecing allowances. Review Skirt Piecing and Piecing Allowance, pages 90–92, for more information about when to use, and how to calculate, piecing allowances. While it isn't a part of the finished, pieced skirt, this can help you more accurately determine how many full-width panels you'll need to make the skirt and, therefore, the fabric yardage requirements.

Calculating Your Skirt Measurements

This table provides an easy reference for the additional pleat and gathering allowances needed for each basic skirt style.

	LENGTH	WIDTH (PERIMETER +1")	
SKIRT			
SKIRT TYPE		**PLEAT/GATHER ALLOWANCE (ADD TO PERIMETER AND SEAM ALLOWANCE)**	**TOTAL**
Flat skirt		4" (1" × 4)	
Corner box or inverted pleats (6")		48" (12" × 4)	
Corner knife pleats (3")		24" (6" × 4)	
Allover knife pleats (3")		(6" × number of pleats)	
Corner gathers		24" (6" × 4)	
Fully gathered skirt		Perimeter (total of 2× perimeter)	

HEMS

WHILE A STRAIGHT 2" hem is standard, you have a variety of ways to finish the hems of your slipcovers. Here are some options for you to consider.

Sewing a Standard Hem

For a standard straight 2" hem, add a 2½" hem allowance, in addition to a ½" seam allowance, for a total of 3" allowance in the cut skirt-panel length. Fold and press the bottom edge of the pieced skirt ½" to the wrong side. Fold and press the bottom edge again, 2" to the wrong side. Stitch close to the inner folded edge.

Sewing a Scalloped Hem

For a scalloped hem, add 1" to the length for a combined hem and seam allowance. In addition, cut and piece a facing the same width as the skirt, and 1½" taller than the finished scallops.

1. Make a paper scallop template using a *French curve* (a plastic template to draft curves for sewing patterns), plate, or similar rounded edge. To determine the size and shape of the scallops, consider how tall (deep) you want the finished scallops to be and the full width of the finished skirt. Also consider if you want the scallops to meet at the furniture's corners, as illustrated on page 76, or if this detail is not necessary.

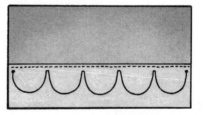

2. Fold and press the top raw edge of the facing ½" to the wrong side and stitch. Stack facing and skirt right sides together and align the bottom raw edges. Baste the bottom edge with a scant ½" seam allowance.

3. Use the scallop template to trace the stitching lines on the facing, across the entire width of the skirt, with the bottom edge of the scallops just above the basting line. Carefully stitch the marked lines, pivoting where scallops meet.

4. Trim the seam allowance close to the stitching, trimming the seams with pinking shears, or *notching the curves* (cutting frequently). Clip right up to, but not through, the stitching line where scallops meet. Turn right side out and press.

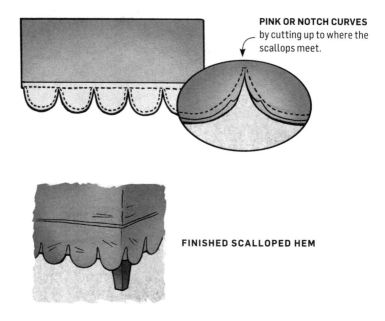

PINK OR NOTCH CURVES by cutting up to where the scallops meet.

FINISHED SCALLOPED HEM

Sewing a Welted Hem

A welted hem refers to a hem that has welting on its finished bottom edge.

The main skirt should be cut to the finished length, plus 1" for a combined hem and seam allowance. Baste welting to the lower skirt edge according to the instructions on pages 29–30. Cut a facing the same full calculated width as the skirt and 1½" long. Fold and press the top raw edge of the facing ½" to the wrong side and stitch. Place the raw edge of the facing on the bottom edge of the skirt, right sides together, welting sandwiched between the layers. Stitch with a zipper foot. Press the facing to the wrong side of the skirt. Slipstitch the facing in place close to the hemmed edge, or use your machine's blind hem stitch settings.

FINISHED WELTED HEM

Bound Hem

You can also bind the bottom edge of the skirt with double-fold bias binding. The skirt should be cut to the finished length, plus ½" for a seam allowance. Bias binding is typically available in ½" or ¾" widths at the fabric store, or you can make your own. Start by cutting and sewing the bias strips, then attach them to the bottom edge of your skirt using one of the two methods described on the following pages.

MAKING AND ATTACHING BIAS STRIPS

1. To make your own, use the instructions in Making Bias Strips (see pages 20–24) to make bias strips that are 2" wide (for ½" bias binding) or 3" wide (for ¾" bias binding), using either the Strip Piecing or Continuous Loop method.

2. Fold and press the bias strip in half lengthwise, wrong sides facing, aligning the raw edges.

3. Open the strip and press the long raw edges on both sides into the crease. Press both short ends in ½".

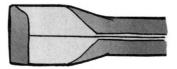

4. Refold along the original crease and press.

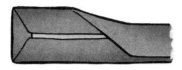

ATTACHING BIAS STRIPS, METHOD 1

1. For this traditional method, unfold the bias binding and press one short end ½" to the wrong side. Starting at the folded short edge, pin the bias binding in place along the raw edge of the piece to be bound, with right sides together. Stitch along the pressed crease, using a ½" seam allowance for ½" double-fold bias binding, or ¾" for ¾" double-fold bias binding. Overlap the ends by ½" and trim away the excess binding.

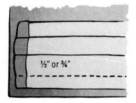

½" or ¾"

(continued on next page)

2. Refold the bias binding along the original creased fold lines, folding it over to the wrong side of the piece being bound, thus encasing the raw edge.

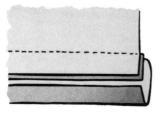

REFOLD THE BIAS BINDING along the original creased fold lines.

3. Press, pin, and stitch the binding in place close to the inner folded edge.

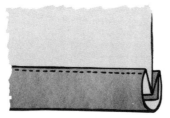

FOLD OVER TO THE WRONG SIDE, encasing raw edge, and stitch.

ATTACHING BIAS STRIPS, METHOD 2

1. This easy method works best with manufactured and prefolded bias tape. Slip the bias binding over the bottom raw edge of the skirt, encasing the raw edge completely. If using packaged bias tape, you will notice that one half of the bias tape is slightly narrower than the other; this narrower edge should be placed on the right side of the fabric.

2. Working from the right side of the project, topstitch the binding in place close to the folded edge of the binding. Stitching on the narrower edge on the right side helps ensure you will catch the wider edge on the wrong side in the stitching line.

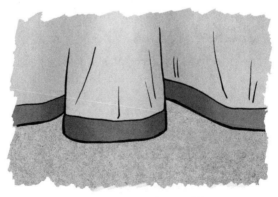

FINISHED BOUND HEM

CHAPTER SEVEN

YARDAGE REQUIREMENTS

You're almost ready to go! But before purchasing your fabric and delving in, of course you need to know how to calculate total yardage requirements. Learn how pattern repeats, piecing seam allowances, and railroading techniques affect the amount of fabric required. Check out some sample cutting layouts and try your hand at drafting your own.

THINGS TO CONSIDER

THE BEST WAY TO DETERMINE the specific fabric requirements for your slipcover is to take all measurements, draft them to scale on graph paper, and plan a cutting layout according to the width of the selected fabric. While you can find broad yardage estimates for different furniture pieces in many how-tos, these can be too wide-ranging to be useful, not to mention potentially misleading; after all, there are so many variables based on the specific dimensions of each pattern piece, skirt style, and more.

For instance, in contrast to a flat skirt or no skirt at all, a full-length, fully gathered skirt adds significantly to your yardage requirements. Seat and back cushion covers add further to yardage needs, so decide *before* the measuring process if you are creating cushion covers or if, instead, the slipcover will cover the cushions as well as the upholstered frame.

On the other hand, sometimes you need even the broadest yardage estimates to aid in cost calculations during your initial shopping trips, if only to help inform the fabric selection process. You may not yet have finalized a skirt style or fabric width, as the cost impacts of these may ultimately factor into your decisions. I have provided some ballpark yardage estimates for different slipcovers, as well as some sample cutting layouts (see pages 84, 118–121), primarily to show how the width of the fabric, and cutting on grain or railroading, can impact yardage needs. These sample layouts show abutted pattern pieces, as they assume you are working with the final measurements.

Please remember that when marking and cutting your muslin, you should allow for and cut out an *extra 2" fitting allowance around each edge of every individual piece*.

Once you're done with the fitting process and you're ready to mark and cut pieces from the final fabric, you *can* abut the fabric pieces in your cutting layout unless you need to match pattern repeats. If you need to match pattern repeats, please consult Pattern Repeats (see pages 85–88) *before* purchasing and cutting your fabric, since this process can significantly impact overall yardage requirements *and* pattern piece placement.

BALLPARKING YARDAGE

THE MEASUREMENTS BELOW are *rough* estimates for the yardage typically needed for different types of slipcovers. *Again, pattern repeat matching is not considered.* These estimates assume a basic flat skirt with corner pleats or gathers; for a fully gathered or pleated skirt, your yardage requirements may be quite a bit more.

Estimating Yardage Needs

FURNITURE TYPE	60" WIDE	54" WIDE	45" WIDE
Ottoman	1–3 yds	2–4 yds	2–5 yds
Straight chair	2–7 yds	3–9 yds	4–10 yds
Armchair	3–10 yds	4–12 yds	5–15 yds
Loveseat (up to 60" wide)	8–12 yds	10–15 yds	12–20 yds
Sofa (60"–90" wide)	12–18 yds	15–22 yds	15–25 yds

PATTERN REPEATS

FOR A PROFESSIONAL LOOK, match the *repeat* (a printed design that is repeated at regular intervals across the width and down the length of the fabric) when seaming slipcover pieces together. This is particularly important if you've chosen a directional design that can't be railroaded, and you need to piece together panels to form whole pattern pieces. Even when you don't need to piece a whole pattern piece together (such as when railroading), you may want to consider and match repeats at seams where one surface plane of the furniture meets another; for instance, where boxing strips meet skirts and where inside arms meet outside arms, just to name two. By matching the repeats in these places, you will minimize the visibility of the seams in your slipcover and give your furniture, and therefore your whole home, a cohesive and polished look.

When matching pattern repeats, there are two main considerations: how to figure the extra yardage needed when you're at the fabric store, and then how to physically match them during the cutting and seaming process.

Determining Yardage for Pattern Repeats

Accounting for repeats is a little more complicated for slipcovers than for other home-decor items, such as curtains, because seams run both vertically and horizontally on a three-dimensional slipcover. This means that you have to account for both the horizontal repeat and the vertical repeat. Trying to precisely calculate yardage requirements based on the specific, individual vertical and horizontal measurements would drive you more than a little batty, because they depend on both the exact measurements of your slipcover parts *and* how those compare to the repeat measurements.

Luckily, we have a handy-dandy rule of thumb to help you estimate the additional fabric you'll need! For best results, sketch your cutting layout on graph paper to determine what your yardage requirements would be *if* pattern repeat wasn't a consideration (see pages 118–121). You'd want to know this anyway before shopping for fabric.

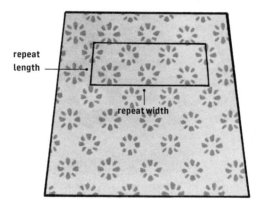

MEASURING A REPEAT

Once you've picked out your preferred fabric, measure the repeat horizontally and then measure it vertically. Note that you aren't measuring just a motif on the fabric, but the full print that is repeated. This may encompass a larger surface area than is apparent at first glance. Add these measurements together, then use the table below to determine the percentage of extra fabric to buy. For example, if the repeat measures 12" vertically and 18" horizontally, add 12" + 18" = 30". The percentage is higher for 45" wide fabric, due to its narrower width and consequently, the fewer possible repeats across the width.

Pattern Repeat Allowance

REPEAT TOTAL (LENGTH + WIDTH)	45" WIDTH % OF EXTRA FABRIC REQUIRED	54"/60" WIDTH % OF EXTRA FABRIC REQUIRED
0"–4"	10	0
5"–9"	20	5
10"–14"	30	10
15"–19"	35	15
20"–24"	40	20
25"–29"	45	25
30"–39"	50	30
40"–50"	55	40

Matching Repeats

Once you have the right amount of fabric, how do you go about matching the repeats at the seams? As emphasized before, it is extremely important to use a muslin cut a little larger than your furniture measurements to finalize pattern-piece dimensions and seam placement. You can't match repeats if you don't know exactly how the pieces are going to come together.

When you have finalized the exact pattern-piece sizes (see Pinning, Fitting, and Basting, pages 94–96), cut one of the larger, more central (and visible) pattern pieces out of the final fabric. On an ottoman, this might be the platform; on a couch, perhaps the center panel for the inside back. When cutting this first piece out, check the print motif placement to make sure it's positioned on the pattern piece exactly how you'd like it to appear on your finished cover.

Once that panel is cut, you can start matching and cutting neighboring body parts. For a couch, this might be the additional panels needed to piece a full inside back. Start by lightly pressing the ½" seam allowance of the cut piece toward the wrong side. Place the cut panel on top of your fabric yardage, both right sides facing up. The pressed seam allowance should stay folded to the wrong side.

Move and position the cut piece until you match the repeat on the fabric yardage, ensuring you have enough visible fabric to cut the appropriate dimensions of the second piece. Pin the cut piece to the yardage at the fold. Gently unfold the cut piece so right sides of the pattern pieces are together. The seam allowance of the cut piece is now visible, and marks the cut edge of the new piece.

PANEL PIECING TIPS

WHEN YOU NEED TO PIECE TOGETHER a whole pattern panel (for instance, a sofa back that is wider than the fabric width), it's generally best *not* to have a vertical seam running down the center of your furniture unless you're planning to make the seam a design element (perhaps with welting). Instead, center one piece on the furniture part to be covered, and then piece any additional panels symmetrically on each side. Such off-center seams will be less visible than a center seam. Remember that each seam requires an additional 1" seam allowance per panel. If you're matching pattern repeats, follow the instructions in Matching Repeats (see page 88) when cutting additional panels. If you want to minimize piecing requirements, look for a fabric that allows railroading.

Railroading

Railroading minimizes, though it may not fully eliminate, the need to match repeats at seams or where different parts meet. "Railroading" refers to running the *length* of the fabric across the *width* of the furniture, or in layman's parlance, turning the fabric sideways. If you can railroad your fabric, you won't have to piece a sofa back, no matter how wide the sofa. This works best with solids, checks, tossed (nondirectional) prints, border prints, or prints that are designed selvage to selvage for the purposes of railroading. Stripes, chevrons, and other directional prints could work for railroading, depending on how much you care about print direction.

Skirt Piecing and Piecing Allowance

Although I'm using skirt piecing as the example, the calculations I'm describing are also useful whenever you need to piece a larger slipcover part together, including a boxing or sofa back.

Without a piecing allowance, it's easy to find yourself short on the number (and size) of cut panels required to piece together the slipcover skirt, due to the loss incurred in seam allowances. Here's an example:

You are slipcovering an ottoman with a perimeter of 120" (which includes the 1" seam allowance, as instructed on page 43). You plan to make four corner box pleats and have no need for a zipper closure. You are using a 45"-wide fabric. Using the instructions in Pleats (see pages 66–70), you come up with a finished skirt width of 168":

120" perimeter + 48" pleat allowance = 168" finished skirt width.

Without a piecing allowance calculation, we might assume that we could take the 168" total, divide by the 42" usable fabric width, and get four panels to piece the skirt. However, since we lose 1" per panel due to seam allowances whenever we piece, we actually could fall 4" short, and four panels would not be enough fabric for the perimeter of the skirt.

The *piecing allowance*, then, adds a certain percentage to the skirt width — basically accounting for all those potential pieced seam allowances — *before* you even know how many panels (and seams) you need. It's not a precise science, but it should prevent a mini disaster like the one described above. Since the number of panels you need to assemble the skirt can vary depending on the usable width of the fabric, so does the piecing allowance.

- For 45"-wide fabrics, add 3 percent to the calculated width (perimeter, ease/pleating allowance, closure allowance); that is, multiply the skirt width by 1.03. Divide this product by 42" (the actual usable fabric width due to shrinkage and selvages), and round up to the next whole number to calculate the number of panels needed.

- For 54" wide fabrics, add 2.5 percent to the calculated width (perimeter, ease/pleating allowance, closure allowance); that is, multiply the skirt width by 1.025. Divide this product by 52" (the actual usable fabric width due to shrinkage and selvages), and round up to the next whole number to calculate the number of panels needed.

- For 60" wide fabrics, add 2 percent to the calculated width (perimeter, ease/pleating allowance, closure allowance); that is, multiply the skirt width by 1.02. Divide this product by 58" (the actual usable fabric width due to shrinkage and selvages), and round up to the next whole number to calculate the number of panels needed.

To see this in action, let's use the same example as above.

1. Using the piecing allowance for 45"-wide fabrics, we calculate the piecing allowance as follows: 168" (finished skirt width) × 1.03 = 173".

2. Divide this product by the 42" usable width of our fabric, so 173" ÷ 42 = 4.12. Rounding *up* to the next whole number, we determine that we would need *five* panels to piece and complete the skirt.

Determining Actual Cut Width

To figure the actual cut width of all panels, discard the piecing allowance from all future calculations; it's not actually a part of the finished skirt or its cut panels.

SYMMETRICAL APPROACH

If you want all five panels to be the same width, calculate the cut width of each panel like so:

- To the finished full width of the skirt panel, add 1" seam allowance to every panel needed to piece the skirt. Divide that sum by the number of panels needed.

Here's how to figure this with the same example used on page 91:

- 168" (finished width) + 5" (1" seam allowance for each of the five panels) = 173" (to include seam allowances). 173" ÷ 5 = 34.6"; that is, each panel needs to be just over 34½" wide.

SEAM CAMOUFLAGE

On the other hand, you may want to consider where you want the seams to fall for maximum seam camouflage. This may mean that some panels are longer than others, either to match repeats or to hide some seams within pleats. If so, plan the length of the individual skirt pieces accordingly. Since this process would be highly individualized — depending on piece dimensions, skirt style, fabric width, and fabric repeat — I'll simply note that, in this case, you'd still do the calculations to determine total number of skirt panels, cut them across the total width of the fabric, then trim them down as needed during the actual piecing and pleating process.

CHAPTER EIGHT

PROJECTS

The projects in this chapter will walk you through the process of fitting and sewing a slipcover for specific types of furniture. You'll want to cross-reference the instructions in this chapter with the information in previous sections to complete your customized look, one that reflects your personality and style. No matter how hopelessly froufrou that floral chintz hand-me-down sofa may be, all it may take is a few days' work to give it new life. So, now that you have everything else figured out, time to start putting the whole thing together!

PINNING, FITTING, AND BASTING

THESE PINNING AND FITTING INSTRUCTIONS apply to all of the following projects — ottomans, chairs, and sofas — so, before tackling the projects, read through this section first. Remember, *your* furniture's unique shape will dictate the specifics of your pattern piece names, shapes, placement, and construction method. Each individual furniture piece is going to vary from the next: arms might be inside or outside the back frame, for instance. These variations might dictate changes to the fitting and stitching process for any given piece. Be flexible and willing to try new things, and just remember to test as you go.

All steps assume that you're using muslin that contains 2" of fitting allowance outside of the original marked lines in the pin-fit process. The skirt does not typically need to be cut or tested with muslin, unless you'd prefer to do so (to confirm seam and pleat dimensions and placement).

Before you start the testing and fitting process, make sure that all individual pattern pieces are already assembled if piecing was necessary — in other words, if the pattern piece needed was wider than the fabric. These might include, but aren't limited to, boxing, skirt, platform, and sofa back. Refer to Panel Piecing Tips (see pages 89–91) for specific tips and tricks on the process of piecing a single pattern piece.

1. Be sure to mark the right and wrong sides of the muslin during the fitting and pinning process. This is particularly important if furniture is assymetrical. (Muslin can be fitted wrong side out if the piece is symmetrical. If it is asymmetrical it must be fitted right side out.)

2. Make sure all muslin pieces extend at least 1" past the intended seamline before pinning to the furniture with T-pins. The seam allowances of any adjoining muslin on the furniture should be folded back and away from the adjoining seam.

3. Once muslin is pinned to furniture, mark any new seam placements as needed using a contrasting ink color. Label each seam, for example, "upper back to inside back," "top arm to front arm," and so on.

4. For darts, tucks, and other similar markings, you may wish to use yet another color or a different kind of marking line to differentiate those from construction seams joining two pieces.

5. Remove pins from the furniture, using them to pin muslin pieces together at the seams before removing the muslin from the furniture.

6. *Baste* all seams (stitch together using the longest stitch length possible) in the test muslin; you'll need to disassemble them later to use the muslin pieces as patterns for the finished slipcover. Baste seams step-by-step, after fitting each new pattern piece, rather than all at once.

7. Once you are satisfied with the fit, mark the final seams and trim the excess fabric, leaving ½" seam allowance outside the final marked lines on every piece. Pay attention to RS/WS markings during the stitching and final fitting process.

8. Test the final fit of the muslin before disassembling and using the finalized muslin pieces as patterns to construct the slipcover from your final fabric.

9. Once you've stitched and tested the fit of the final slipcover, finish all seam allowances (see Finessing Seams, page 26).

Supplies and Tools

Specific supplies (welting, trims, zippers, batting, etc.) will vary according to your desired slipcover (like fabric yardage does), so those are not all included in the projects that follow. But there are some basic sewing items you'll need when making any type of slipcover. Here's a short list of what to have on hand:

- sewing machine and appropriate needles and bobbins
- muslin
- graph paper and pencil
- sharp fabric-cutting shears
- pinking shears
- rotary cutter and mat
- tape measure, ruler, and yardstick
- T-square or carpenter's square

- marking tools (disappearing-ink fabric marker, chalk, etc., in at least two contrasting colors)
- T-pins or upholstery pins
- straight pins
- point turner
- seam ripper
- hand-sewing needles
- iron and ironing board

RECTANGULAR OTTOMAN SLIPCOVER

Ottomans are a great first slipcover project. Piecing tends to be simple, and you can make a huge difference in the look of a piece with a small(ish) amount of effort. Through the creative use of drops and/or boxing strips, trims, and skirt styling, you can make this project your own!

PIN AND FIT

1. **Platform.** Center the muslin pattern on the ottoman platform and smooth it out from the center. Pin in place, starting at the center of each side and working toward the corners.

   If creating a drop, smooth the fabric from the center and toward the corners down over the top edges. Create darts in each corner where two dropped edges meet.

   Fit, pin, and mark your planned seam placement. If you created a drop, remove the platform and baste the darts before replacing the muslin on the platform and adding the boxing.

2. **Boxing.** (This step is optional if platform includes a drop.) Lay the boxing on the sides of the ottoman, positioning piecing seams as desired. Make sure the boxing hangs straight on the furniture. As you fit, pin, and mark the joining seams, take care the fabric doesn't shift.

3. **Baste muslin together.** Trim any excess fabric from the pinned seams, leaving a ½" seam allowance. Remove the muslin from the furniture, pinning the panels together

(continued on next page)

before removing them, and baste the boxing to the platform. Pivot seams ½" from each corner.

Place the muslin back on the ottoman, as before. If the bottom edges of the muslin pieces aren't even, now is the time to trim everything to match. Measuring up from the floor all around, mark the line at which the skirt will attach. Trim, leaving a ½" seam allowance.

ASSEMBLE THE SLIPCOVER

1. Once you're satisfied with the fit of the muslin, begin dismantling the basted pattern pieces with a seam ripper. Be careful not to distort the fabric in the process. Label all seams with a fabric marker to ensure proper cutting and assembly of the final pieces.

2. Use the muslin patterns to cut slipcover pieces from the final fabric, matching pattern repeats or positioning fabric motifs before cutting, as desired (see pages 85–88).

3. Baste the welting (see pages 29–30) to top and/or bottom edges of boxing before assembly, as desired.

4. Stitch the fabric pieces together in the order you stitched the muslin pieces. Test the fit once more before attaching the skirt.

ATTACH THE SKIRT

Measure the perimeter of the completed slipcover. Piece and hem your desired skirt style, following the instructions on pages 74–77. Stitch completed skirt to the slipcover.

ROUND STOOL SLIPCOVER

Like a rectangular ottoman, round stools are a nice and easy intro to slipcovers due to the minimal "body parts" and ease of construction. Play with skirt length, deciding if you want to completely hide the legs or allow them to peek out.

PIN AND FIT

1. **Platform.** Start by fitting and shaping the platform. Make four marks around the platform edge, dividing it into quarters. If creating a drop, gather the fabric at the raw edge, or create a series of evenly spaced tucks or darts to ease in the fullness (see page 28). Gathering is the easiest and quickest approach; use the dental floss and zigzag stitch method within each of the four quarter-sections (see page 72). Place and center the muslin on the ottoman platform, pinning in place at the center and working out toward the edges of the platform. Check the placement of the tucks or pull the floss in each section to gather, so you can check the fit and distribution around the ottoman. Fit, pin, and mark seam placement.

2. **Boxing.** If you created a drop on the platform, mark the boxing into four equal segments before placing it on the ottoman. Lay the boxing around the ottoman, making sure the boxing hangs straight. Line up the four marks on the boxing with those on the platform.

   As you fit, pin, and mark seams, be careful the fabric doesn't shift.

(continued on next page)

3. **Baste muslin together.** Trim any excess fabric from the pinned seams, leaving a ½" seam allowance. Remove the muslin from the furniture, pinning the pieces together before removing them, and baste the boxing to the platform. Keep any gathers evenly distributed around the circumference, if applicable.

    Place the muslin back on the ottoman. If the bottom edges of the muslin panels aren't even, now is the time to trim everything to match. Measuring up from the floor all around, mark the line at which the skirt will attach. Trim, leaving a ½" seam allowance.

ASSEMBLE THE SLIPCOVER

1. Once you're satisfied with the fit of the muslin, begin dismantling the pattern pieces with a seam ripper; be careful not to distort the fabric in the process. Label all seams with fabric marker to ensure proper cutting and assembly of the final slipcover pieces.

2. Use the muslin patterns to cut slipcover pieces from the final fabric, matching pattern repeats or positioning fabric motifs before cutting, as desired (see pages 85–88).

3. Baste the welting (see pages 29–30) to top and/or bottom edges of boxing before assembly, as desired.

4. Stitch the fabric pieces together in the order you stitched the muslin pieces. Test the fit once more before attaching the skirt.

ATTACH THE SKIRT

Measure the perimeter of the completed slipcover. Piece and hem your desired skirt style, following instructions on pages 74–77. Stitch completed skirt to the slipcover.

STRAIGHT CHAIR SLIPCOVER

Chairs without arms tend to be simpler and less diverse than armchairs and sofas, but size, shape, and construction can still vary. While I provide one possible assembly order here, you may find that another process works better for your own chair. No matter how you piece things together, you may find areas where two seams, running in opposite directions, meet. In such a case, be sure that you don't stitch into an adjoining seam, and pivot fabrics and seams when stitching in a different direction. Take a deep breath, review the general pinning and fitting process instructions, and get going! Straight chairs make a great first or second slipcover project.

PIN AND FIT

1. **Inside back/outside back.** Baste together the top raw edges of the inside and outside back muslins. Drape them over the back of the chair, aligning the seam at the upper back edge. Center them side to side, making sure the muslin hangs straight. Smooth out from the center, moving to each side. Fit, pin, and mark seams if inside back is wrapping around and forming the sides of the back.

(continued on next page)

2. **Back Gussets.** If applicable, place the gussets on each side of the chair, making sure the pieces hang straight. Fit, pin, and mark seam placement.

   Trim excess fabric and then baste gussets to inside/ outside back; place back on chair, inside out.

3. **Platform.** Drape the platform muslin over the seat. If you included a tuck-in allowance at the inside back and platform (for fully upholstered chairs only; see page 47), make sure these are the same length, mark the tuck-in allowance, then fold and pin both tuck-ins out of the way. Make sure the platform muslin is straight on the seat. Start in the center and smooth out toward the corners. If it contains front or side drops, fold edges over and down. Fit, pin, and mark corner darts as needed. Remove from chair.

   Baste darts in the drop, if applicable, and baste plat-form to inside back (and back gussets, if applicable).

4. **Boxing.** Place slipcover back on chair. Place the boxing strip(s) on the sides of the chair, making sure the boxing hangs straight. Line up piecing seams as desired. Fit, pin, and mark seams.

   If the bottom edges of the muslin pieces aren't even, now is the time to trim everything to match. Measuring up from the floor all around, mark the line at which the skirt will attach, if adding, and trim to even up, leaving a ½" seam allowance.

ASSEMBLE THE SLIPCOVER

1. Once you're satisfied with the fit of the muslin, begin dismantling the pattern pieces with a seam ripper; be careful not to distort the fabric in the process. Label all seams with fabric marker to ensure proper cutting and assembly of the final slipcover pieces.

2. Use the muslin patterns to cut slipcover pieces from the final fabric, matching pattern repeats or positioning fabric motifs before cutting, as desired (see pages 85–88).

3. Baste the welting (see pages 29–30) to back gussets and top and bottom edges of boxing before assembly, as desired.

4. Stitch the fabric pieces together in the order you stitched the muslin pieces. Test the fit once more before attaching the skirt. If you don't want a skirt, hem the bottom edge of the slipcover as desired.

ATTACH THE SKIRT

Measure the perimeter of the completed slipcover. Piece and hem your desired skirt style, following instructions on pages 74–77. Stitch completed skirt to the slipcover.

ARMCHAIR OR SOFA SLIPCOVER

Since sofas are basically just very long and oversized armchairs, the same instructions apply to both — they each have exactly the same body parts and process steps. The main difference is in the size, overall yardage requirements, and the additional seaming and piecing that may be needed in larger pieces.

PIN AND FIT

1. **Inside back and back gussets.** Start by fitting and shaping the inside back panel. This is the part that most determines the structure of the slipcover as a whole, and it will take the most shaping (other than the arms). Find the center top and bottom edges of the chair/sofa inside back and of the muslin pattern piece, and pin them together at the center points.

   Smooth out the muslin from the center points. Drape the muslin up and over the top edge, at least 1" past the top seam; pin in place. Next, work toward and around the

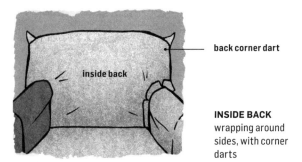

back corner dart

INSIDE BACK
wrapping around
sides, with corner
darts

sides. If you don't have a back gusset pattern piece, drape the inside back around the sides and toward the back seam. In this case, form, pin, and mark darts or tucks at the upper back edges to work out the excess fabric (see page 28).

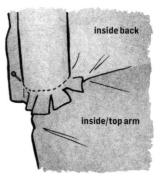

If you created back gussets, place them on each side, making sure they hang straight on the furniture. Start at the top center and work your way out and down on each side. Fit, pin, and mark seams.

There are many ways the inside back (and back gussets) could meet the arms, so rather than try to encompass all the possibilities here, I'll boil it down to the essential points. Wrap the inside back muslin (and back gussets, if applicable) around the inside/top arm, clipping, notching, and trimming the muslin as needed so that the fabric lies flat against the furniture frame. When trimming excess, be sure to keep the ½" seam allowances. Fit, pin, and mark seams.

At the bottom of the inside back, mark the top of the tuck-in allowance. Trim the bottom edge as needed to match your desired tuck-in allowance (3", for instance). (See What is a Tuck-In Allowance? on page 47.)

(continued on next page)

2. **Inside arms and top arms.** If the top arms are separate pieces from the inside arms, baste them together at the top edges before pinning and fitting. Again, there are many different ways to shape and join arms to the inside back. Drape the inside/top arm pieces over each arm, making sure they hang straight on the furniture. Fit, pin, and mark seams.

    If the inside/top arms wrap around the front, mark and make tucks or darts to work out the excess fabric (see page 28). Fit, pin, and mark all seams. At the bottom of the inside arms, mark the top of the tuck-in allowance. Trim the bottom edge as needed to fit your desired tuck-in allowance.

    Clip any corners and curves within the seam allowance. Cut away any excess fabric beyond the ½" seam allowance much as you did for the back's upper corners.

3. **Front arms.** Lay the front arm panels on the front of each arm, making sure they hang straight on the furniture. Fit, pin, and mark seams. Be careful the fabric doesn't shift; start at the top center and work your way out and down on each side. Note that the front arm may extend past the top of the inside arm tuck-in allowance; if so, the bottom of the front arm will be basted to the platform drop or boxing at a later step.

front arm

4. **Baste inner slipcover together.** Pin the muslin pieces together at the seams in this order before removing: inside back to back gussets (if applicable), inside/back gussets to inside/top arms (as applicable), and inside/top arms to front arms. Trim any excess fabric, leaving a ½" seam allowance.

    Remove muslin from the furniture and baste together in this order:
    - tucks and darts at upper back corners
    - inside back to back gussets (if applicable)
    - inside back/gussets to inside/top arms
    - inside/top arms to front arms, making sure to stop at the top of the inside arm tuck-in allowance

5. **Platform/front boxing.** If your slipcover contains a front boxing strip instead of a drop, baste the front edge of the platform muslin to the top edge of the boxing muslin, centering the boxing on the front platform edge (the platform contains tuck-in allowances on each side; the boxing doesn't). If your boxing wraps around the sides and/or the back instead, add this just before the skirt at a later step.

    Place the slipcover back on the furniture. Fold the tuck-in allowances of the inside back and inside arms up and away from the platform and temporarily pin those out of the way.

    Find the center of the furniture platform at the front and back edge, as well as the center of the muslin pattern

(continued on next page)

piece. Align the center points and pin in place. If the platform is T-shaped or L-shaped or otherwise has interior corners, trim and clip the inner corners within the seam allowance to help the muslin lie flat against the furniture frame.

If there is a drop, smooth and shape the platform down at the front and the corners, pinning and marking any darts or tucks necessary for shaping (see page 28). Trim as necessary in the front to eliminate excess tuck-in allowance where it isn't necessary (where the furniture doesn't have a tuck-in crevice, such as where the front frame attaches to the arms).

Fold the tuck-in allowances at the back and sides up and away from the seams. Mark the top of the tuck-in allowances and trim the bottom edge as needed, taking care that all allowances are of equal depth.

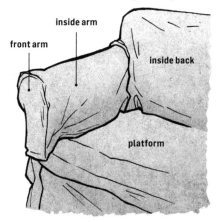

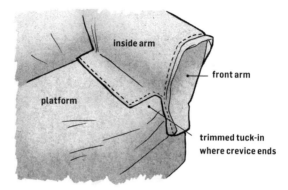

inside arm

front arm

platform

trimmed tuck-in
where crevice ends

6. **Outside arms.** Lay the outside arm panels on each arm, making sure they hang straight on the furniture. Fit, pin, and mark seams. Be careful the fabric doesn't shift; start at the top center and work your way out and down.

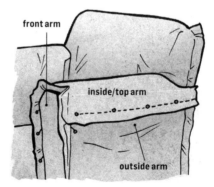

front arm

inside/top arm

outside arm

(continued on next page)

7. **Continue basting.** Pin the platform and outside arms to the rest of the slipcover before removing from the furniture, trimming excess fabric while leaving tuck-in and seam allowances in place. Remove the muslin pieces and baste together in this order:
   - back edge of platform to inside back
   - side edges of platform to inside arms
   - platform/boxing to front arms
   - outside arms to inside/top arms
   - outside arms to front arms

   Depending on the shape and construction of your furniture, you may have multiple seams intersecting and fabrics changing directions (for instance, if the platform contains a drop or is T- or L-shaped). Clip and pivot seam allowances and fabrics as necessary, and be sure not to stitch into an adjoining seam.

8. **Back arms.** If the arms are attached outside of the back frame, you may have separate back arm pieces. Fit, pin, and mark seams just as for the outside arms. Baste to outer and inside/top arms before joining outside back.

9. **Outside back.** Place the muslin slipcover back on the furniture as before. Center the muslin on the outside back, pinning it at the center top and bottom edge. Fit, pin, and mark seams. Be careful the fabric doesn't shift; start at the center and work your way out and down.

If inserting a zipper closure, leave full 1" *seam allowances* on one vertical edge, such as where the outside back and outer (or back) arm meet. Remove from furniture and baste outside back to slipcover all around, leaving the seam with the 1" seam allowance open (if applicable).

Test the fit one last time. If the bottom edges of the muslin pieces don't line up, now is the time to trim everything up. Measuring up from the floor all around, mark the line at which the skirt (or all-around boxing strip, if applicable) will attach and trim, leaving the ½" seam allowance.

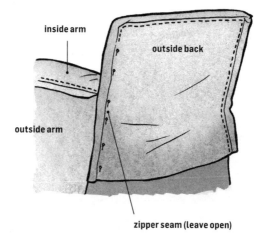

inside arm

outside back

outside arm

zipper seam (leave open)

(continued on next page)

ASSEMBLE THE SLIPCOVER

1. Once you're satisfied with the fit of the muslin, begin dismantling the pattern pieces with a seam ripper; be careful not to distort the fabric in the process. Label all seams with fabric marker to ensure proper cutting and assembly of the final slipcover pieces.

2. Use the muslin patterns to cut slipcover pieces from the final fabric, matching pattern repeats or positioning fabric motifs before cutting, as desired (see pages 85–88).

3. Baste the welting (see pages 29–30) to pieces before assembly, as desired.

4. Stitch the fabric pieces together in the same order you stitched the muslin pieces. Test the final fit partway through the assembly process.

ATTACH THE BOXING/SKIRT

1. Measure the perimeter of the completed slipcover.

2. If adding an all-around boxing, piece it and add welting to top and bottom edges as desired. Stitch it to the bottom edge of the slipcover, starting and ending at the zipper closure opening, if applicable.

3. Piece and hem your desired skirt style, following instructions on pages 74–77. Stitch completed skirt to the slipcover, starting and ending at the zipper closure opening, if applicable.

ZIPPERED SEAT CUSHION OR BACK CUSHION

You certainly can make a slipcover that covers not just the furniture frame but any seat and back cushions, too. This is how most retail off-the-shelf slipcovers are designed. However, you'll wind up with a better fit and a less "slipcover-y" look if you design your cover to fit over the frame, with separate covers for the box cushions. Here's how!

Refer to the Cushions section in chapter 5 for specific instructions on measuring each part of the cushion (see pages 58–62). Take measurements for *all* cushions individually, as they may vary. These are the pieces you should have to construct each cushion:

Main panels (2). These will be top/bottom panels for a seat cushion; front/back panels for a back cushion. The length and width of each panel should equal the length and width of the cushion at the widest point plus 1" for seam allowances. Remember that if the cushion is irregularly or asymmetrically shaped, these two panels should be mirror images of each other.

Zipper panel (1). Cut height should equal the thickness of the cushion plus 2"; cut width should equal the length of the existing cushion zipper plus 2". In most cases, this should fit within the full width of your fabric; however, you might need to piece it if your cushion is oversized.

Cushion boxing (1; possibly pieced). Cut height equals the thickness of the cushion plus 1"; cut width equals the cushion perimeter minus the zipper panel, plus 4" for ease and seam allowances. If this exceeds the width of your fabric, piece the boxing from multiple panels.

(continued on next page)

If the cushion boxing width is *less* than twice the width of your fabric, cut *two* boxing panels across the width of the fabric. Keep one whole and call it the *main boxing strip*. Cut the other in half, and stitch each half to the ends of the main boxing strip. Trim as needed to equal the cut cushion boxing width.

If the cushion boxing width is *more* than twice the width of your fabric, cut *three* boxing panels across the width of the fabric. Stitch all three together, end to end. Trim the two end panels as needed to equal the cushion boxing width, while keeping them symmetrical.

Upholstery-weight zipper or zipper chain. This should be as long as or longer than the zipper panel width. Upholstery zipper chain comes without a pull or any stops.

Zipper pull and zipper stop. Using upholstery zipper chain requires that the chains, pulls, and stops be purchased separately and assembled prior to use.

CREATE THE ZIPPER PANEL

1. Cut zipper to fit the width of the zipper panel. If using upholstery zipper chain, slide a zipper pull onto the chain at one end. Slide the pull up and down the length of the zipper to align the zipper teeth, being careful not to pull it all the way down and off the chain. Attach the zipper stop ½" from the closed, bottom end of the zipper. Secure the top end of the zipper with a bar tack (a zigzag stitch back and forth with a 0mm stitch length) to secure the zipper pull and prevent it from coming off the chain later.

2. Fold the zipper panel in half lengthwise, right sides together, and baste ½" away from the fold. Cut the halves apart along the folded edge. Press panels and seam allowance open. Place the zipper panel wrong side up on your work surface.

3. Center the zipper on the basted seam, right side down (wrong sides of zipper and panel are both facing up toward you). Using a zipper foot, stitch along both sides of the zipper tape and across both ends. When stitching across the zipper coil, lift your foot off the pedal and carefully turn the handwheel manually to avoid broken needles or a protesting machine. Flip the zipper panel to the right side and topstitch ⅛" away from each seam to reinforce. Rip the basting stitches out to expose the zipper.

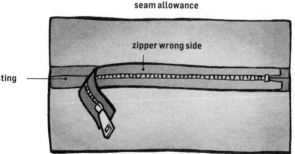

seam allowance

zipper wrong side

basting

ATTACHING a cushion zipper

(continued on next page)

ASSEMBLE THE CUSHION BOXING

1. **Attach the zipper panel.** Stitch the short ends of the zipper panel to the short ends of the cushion boxing, right sides together. Test fit around the circumference of the cushion. If there is any excess, distribute it evenly on either side of the zipper panel and tuck it under each end of the zipper panel. Pin, remove it from the cushion, and baste the excess to the wrong side of the zipper panel along the top and bottom raw edges, within the ½" seam allowance.

2. **Attach the welting.** Baste welting all around the raw edges of both main panels following the Inserting Trims instructions (see pages 29–30).

3. **Attach the boxing.** Pin the assembled boxing to one main panel, right sides facing, centering the zipper panel on the back (or bottom) edge. Stitch all around, clipping the boxing at the corners and any additional curves to ease. To help line up all main corner panels, clip the boxing on the opposite unstitched raw edge, directly across from the clips in the stitched seam allowance. This will mark the best placement for the corners of the second main panel.

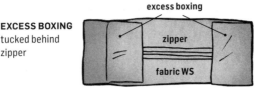

EXCESS BOXING tucked behind zipper

excess boxing

zipper

fabric WS

COMPLETE THE CUSHION

Open the zipper halfway. Pin the second main panel to the boxing, right sides facing, aligning the clipped corners of the boxing strip with the main panel corners. Stitch all around, clipping any additional curves for ease. Finish seams as desired and turn right side out. Remove cushion from old cover, insert into the new cover, and zip up.

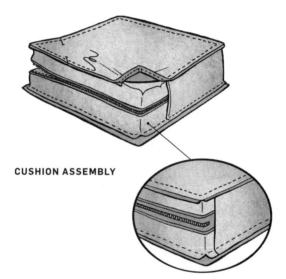

CUSHION ASSEMBLY

APPENDIX

Sample Cutting Layouts

To demonstrate how yardage requirements and cutting layouts can vary depending on fabric width and the on-grain vs. rail-roading decision, I drafted pattern pieces for a slipcover that would drape over the back and seat cushions of an armchair. Two layouts illustrate the yardage I would need if using 54" fabric, with on-grain vs. railroading layouts, as this seems to be a common width for home déc–weight fabrics these days. Remember that your own layouts and yardage needs can vary widely depending on the size and shape of the individual pattern pieces, the need to match pattern repeats, and so forth.

- To draft a sample cutting layout, I recommend you use a few sheets of graph paper. Use one full sheet (or multiple sheets taped together if necessary) to represent the fabric yardage. Determine the scale of each square — does it equal 1", 2", or etc.? Whatever the scale, be sure to mark the fabric width and yardage on the graph paper.

- Use a separate sheet to cut out representations of each pattern piece, using the same scale as the yardage sheet(s). Be sure to indicate the vertical direction on each piece. These cutouts will allow you to position and reposition the pieces in different configurations, to determine the best use of your fabric. As you play with on-grain and railroaded layouts, use the vertical direction indicators to be sure all pieces are facing the same direction (if the fabric pattern, weave, or nap requires it). If you're still undecided on a fabric width, you may need to create a few sample yardage representations, one for each of the different possible widths.

Allow for Shrinkage

While fabrics might be advertised as being 44/45", 54", or 60", the actual usable width of the fabric, once it is prewashed and preshrunk and selvages are trimmed, is usually a few inches less. As you plan your own cutting layouts, assume a 42" width for 44/45"-wide fabric; a 52" width for 54"-wide fabric; and a 58"width for 60"-wide fabrics. Our sample cutting layouts assume a 52" usable width.

Standard Metric Conversion Formulas

WHEN THE MEASUREMENT GIVEN IS	TO CONVERT IT TO	MULTIPLY IT BY
yards	meters (m)	0.9144
yards	centimeters (cm)	91.44
inches	centimeters (cm)	2.54
inches	millimeters (mm)	25.4
inches	meters (m)	0.0254

Standard Equivalents

U.S.	METRIC	U.S.	METRIC
⅛ inch	3.20 mm	⅝ inch	1.59 cm
¼ inch	6.35 mm	¾ inch	1.91 cm
⅜ inch	9.50 mm	⅞ inch	2.22 cm
½ inch	1.27 cm	1 inch	2.54 cm

54" CUTTING LAYOUTS ON GRAIN

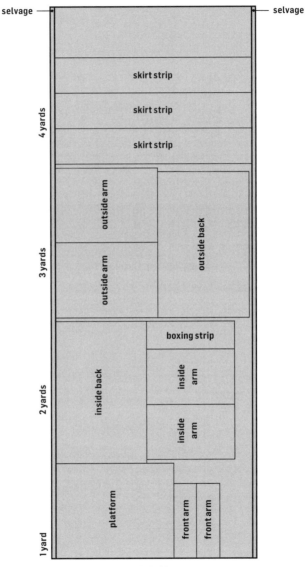

selvage

selvage

4 yards

skirt strip

skirt strip

skirt strip

3 yards

outside arm

outside arm

outside back

2 yards

inside back

boxing strip

inside arm

inside arm

1 yard

platform

front arm

front arm

54" wide

54" CUTTING LAYOUTS RAILROADED

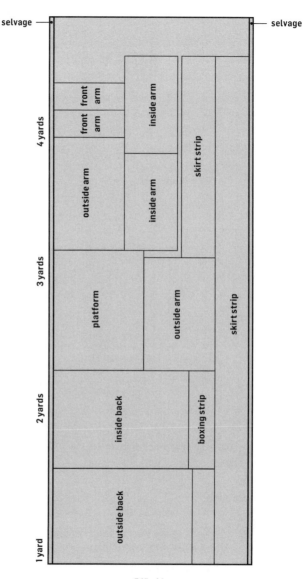

INDEX

Page numbers in *italic* indicate illustrations; page numbers in **bold** indicate charts.